WHY CONTEXT MATTERS

OR, WHERE DID ANGLO-AMERICAN PHILOSOPHY GO WRONG?

Alicia Juarrero

imprint-academic.com

Copyright © Alicia Juarrero, 2025

The moral rights of the author have been asserted.
No part of this publication may be reproduced in any form
without permission, except for the quotation of brief passages
in criticism and discussion.

Published in the UK by
Imprint Academic Ltd., PO Box 200, Exeter EX5 5YX, UK

Distributed in the USA by
Lightning Source,
La Vergne, TN 37086, USA

ISBN 9781788361378 paperback

A CIP catalogue record for this book is available from the
British Library and US Library of Congress

This product complies with the General Product Safety Regulations
introduced by the European Union in 2024.

EU GPSR Authorised Representative:
LOGOS EUROPE, 9 rue Nicolas Poussin,
17000, LA ROCHELLE, France

E-mail: Contact@logoseurope.eu

For Lydia, the best by far

Contents

Introduction ... 1

Part I

1. The Backstory ... 21
2. Track 1: Knowledge of the External World ... 29
3. Track 2: What is Goodness and How Do We Know it? ... 63

   Interlude ... 88

Part II

4. The Women are Up to Something ... 95

   Conclusion ... 137

   Appendix ... 142

   References ... 152

   Index ... 156

Introduction

Humanity has finally come to accept that no individual species exists in isolation from the others. We now understand that critical—indeed defining—features of living things and ecosystems are revealed only when they are examined *as* integrated with each other and with their environment and culture—when they are embedded in context, that is. Ethology learned that lesson before many other natural sciences: animals caged in zoos act very differently from animals in the wild. It took cytologists longer to discover that cells also behave differently in a petri dish than in their natural tissues. The continuing controversy in sociology, economics, and public policy over "structural" influences on human behavior is evidence that the influence of context on individuals has not yet fully permeated public discourse.

We are only now beginning to acknowledge that integrating individual entities into comprehensive totalities with novel properties can also be a feature of the nonliving world: for example, *synchrony* is a systemic property that arises when processes like swinging metronomes become coordinated in a collective pattern; no one thing is synchronous with itself. *Resonance*, too, emerges only when the *frequency* of one vibrating object matches the natural frequency of a nearby object. Neither resonance nor synchrony is an innate property; snapshots cannot capture *frequency* because it is not an internal property of the thing in question. *Frequency* too is an emergent property; it is the rate at which an event or pattern repeats *over time*. Like an image in an intricate tapestry, or the *trend* of a particular sequence, systemic emergent properties like resonance and frequency are products of constrained interactions among diverse things and processes that have self-organized into more encompassing spatial and/or temporal *wholes*. They are emergent and *relational* features of interactions that have become interdependent with each other and with their context.

Synchrony, resonance, and frequency are just three examples of novel but very real and effective powers that arise when individual processes are integrated into coherent dynamics. They are not particle-like; they are relational and systemic qualities that are distributed in space and persist over time. When self-organization achieves closure, a hierarchy with at least two interrelated levels of organization (components and whole) has been born. Once coalesced, dynamic wholes become the invisible context—the background that goes without saying—within which individual events behave meaningfully. As Koestler (1968) noted about holons, hierarchies themselves are often situated within a context, so at least three levels of organization are usually involved. We dismiss background at our peril because context can be causative—as such: it is the *synchronous* stomping, not just the total number of footfalls, that collapses bleachers. It is the *frequency* of certain metabolic processes that disrupts homeostasis. The sequential order in which Heisenberg matrices are organized has been discovered to matter. Greatly.

Understanding how individual elements integrate to produce novel (*because collective, relational,* and *temporal*) properties has been the focus of complex dynamical systems theory.

Philosophers of science are also beginning to understand that it is *constraints* operating among independent entities, processes, events, species that make them interdependent with one another —and *with* the environment or milieu in which they exist. Novel *relational* properties arise as a function of constraints — relations with qualitatively emergent characteristics that are absent from the individual components (Juarrero 2023). Knowledge of such emergent *networked* and *system-wide* properties — collective dynamics that simply do not exist as independent isolated stuff — can be gleaned only by uncovering *how* such synergies and interlocking relations come to be and work. To fully understand complex systems generally, in other words, we must understand how the cosmos turns independent processes into organized symbionts.

As unremarkable as those sentences sound today, working scientists, philosophers of science, and metaphysicians still continue for the most part to picture the universe and our place in it in terms of minuscule and isolated particles that forcefully collide with one another. Newtonian mechanics bequeathed to us the unexamined presupposition that complex entities and processes can be fully explained and predicted by — reduced to — fundamental minuscule and stand-alone entities (nowadays not atoms but quarks and electrons) and the natural laws that govern *them*. According to this model, reality can be fully explained by *analysis* alone — by breaking down observed phenomena into their fundamental stand-alone elements.

Alas, this model also implies that if reality ontologically bottoms out in isolated and independent particles jostled about by forces, apparent *wholes*—be they organisms, biological niches and habitats; persons, cultures, and other social dynamics; even the biosphere—must have merely derivative reality. Reality bottoms out at the atomic level (ontologically speaking). Worse: if all causal power bubbles up from internal properties of individual particles as they collide in response to universal forces, then apparently unified entities like organisms, ecosystems, and cultures— even control systems such as homeostasis—must also be *epiphenomenal as such*. Their interconnected and interdependent dynamics are just frosting on the cake with no fundamental causal power to change the go of anything. According to the received view, in other words, being embedded in a particular culture or biological niche makes no qualitative difference to the properties and behavior of living things: if all causal power derives bottom-up solely from the essential nature of fundamental particles and the elementary forces acting upon them, then identity is stamped on all entities by the fundamental constituents that comprise their "essential nature."

In biology, recent work in epigenetics has complicated matters: epigenetics, the study of how environmental factors can produce changes in genes without modifying the genetic sequence itself (as the Central Dogma in Biology would suppose) has established that genes become activated or suppressed in response to context and timing, with consequences that can persist across generations. The same amino acids can produce different proteins; neural networks in the brain are shaped and pruned by our acting in the world. Different spatiotemporal contexts can fundamentally alter core properties of individuals embedded in distinctive situations. In this monograph I will argue that contextual embeddedness is significant, and not only for living things: we now understand that there are many complex systems (such as laser beams) that are "nothing but" emergent features of processes coordinated in a particular place and moment. Laser beams are novel properties of interconnected and interdependent photon streams, properties with the power to cut and cauterize, which photon streams individually do not.

Context-dependence, in other words, was dismissed from reality and epistemology because interdependence and interconnectedness had no purchase in philosophy of science. As noted above, the standard conceptual framework in place throughout much of the recent history of Western physics and philosophy held that what appear to be holistic units are in fact derivative realities—specifically, they are derivative because causally powerless. Although most clearly articulated by Newtonian mechanics, this picture was definitively secured—entrenched, in fact—during the first decades of the last century by a school of philosophy called *positivism*. The first part of this monograph will examine how and why the combination of Newtonian mechanics and positivism drove academic philosophy especially in Great Britain and the United States to an unacknowledged intellectual impasse.

As an instructive case study of this history, we will consider how and why luminaries of continental European philosophy (think Bergson, Cassirer, Heidegger, Husserl, Merleau-Ponty, Kierkegaard, Nietzsche, Camus, and Sartre, even Marx) were systematically excluded from the North Atlantic canon of metaphysics, epistemology, and ethics. For more than one hundred years, Anglo-American university philosophy departments lumped together the diverse philosophical schools which many of these thinkers founded—phenomenology, existentialism, structuralism, constructivism, deconstruction, and postmodernism—as *continental philosophy*—and summarily dismissed them all as more literature and psychology than philosophy. French existentialists Sartre and Camus clearly belonged in the literature departments (just ask the Nobel committee!); Americans Ralph Waldo Emerson and Henry David Thoreau as well as Spaniards José Ortega y Gassett and Miguel de Unamuno (along with Frenchman Michel de Montaigne and Russian-born Isaiah Berlin) did not fare much better—they were essayists, not real philosophers. Keep going: most likely because his reductionism bottomed out at the scale of transactions on material production, Karl Marx was often sequestered in political science departments, where Marcuse, Lacan, Gramsci, and Althusser would keep him company a few years later. Sigmund Freud's theory of the superego was excluded from epistemology and relegated to the psychology department along with Köhler's gestalt psychology and Husserl's phenomenology (more on which below). Down the hall but still in the general academic division of social science and not philosophy, Frenchman Auguste Comte's ideas were safely ensconced in a new discipline, sociology, with an even newer subdiscipline, sociology of science, carved out later on for Austrians Paul Feyerabend and Karl Popper, and Frenchman Bruno Latour. More recently, twentieth-century French thinkers like Derrida, Deleuze, and Guattari, not to mention Foucault, to name the most prominent, were likewise dismissed together with Alfred North Whitehead's process philosophy, and for the same reason: they were thought to belong more to psychology or sociology than philosophy.

One needed only to ask students deciding upon a dissertation topic at most universities in Britain and the United States at the time: PhD candidates in the second half of the twentieth century who aimed to specialize in existentialism or "continental philosophy" did so at their professional peril. Even a homegrown American school of philosophy like pragmatism was not taken seriously in its own country—until American philosopher Richard Rorty in the late 1970s returned some respectability to that tradition. Barely.

This is not ancient history. Even today, predominant atomist and essentialist approaches echo a Newtonian and positivist mindset, in physics as well as philosophy (see Gillett 2016; Frank, Gleiser and Thompson 2024). This general conceptual lens is still very much with us: it serves as the backdrop against which we formulate many of our philosophical dilemmas. A central goal of this monograph is to show that anglophone philosophy's longstanding refusal to acknowledge the role and significance of *context-dependence* —especially the possibility that novel properties might emerge in response to context-dependent *constraints* — is an unavoidable corollary of an *atomistic, essentialist, and reductionist* worldview that insists that all the heavy causal lifting take place at the level of particles and elementary forces. As efficient causation.

A second aim of this monograph will be to show how upon closer study it becomes clear that the excluded "continental" authors and schools of thought did have something in common: each in their own way *tried to bring relations with the lived context back into philosophy*. And so I will begin with an overview of the philosophical zeitgeist of the era. My goal is to show how, repeatedly, continental European objections to received positivist theses created an opening in which the lived context might have been taken seriously, metaphysically and epistemologically. But having been stripped of context by the dominance of positivism, North Atlantic logic- and science-informed philosophers did not welcome this approach. Doubtless inspired by positivism's stated intent to emulate physics and thereby formulate a science-informed philosophy—one compatible with the reductionist emphasis on atoms and the forces of efficient causality—professional Anglo-American philosophers instead doubled down on positivism. By mid-century, these *modern* presuppositions about metaphysics and knowledge acquisition had solidified as *the* foundational worldview; its framework had become the background "that goes without saying" (*The Blind Spot* 2024).

In contrast to what was happening in professional philosophy, working physicists on the European continent during the first half of the twentieth century struggled philosophically to make sense of flagrantly context-dependent spookiness popping up in the quantum realm. The schools of continental philosophy that this monograph will examine proposed alternative epistemological and metaethical approaches. Despite the way entangled particles and superposition were already muddling experimental outcomes, however, realist presuppositions borrowed from Newtonian science proved too convincing to discard. Einstein explicitly renounced positivism but his realist metaphysics presupposed an ontology that bottoms out in localized particles—only that understanding of ontology could subtend a natural realism, Einstein believed. As a result, self-described positivists like physicists Max Born and Werner Heisenberg explicitly refused to turn away from that philosophical worldview. Anglo-American philosophers followed suit, holding fast to the belief that in the end the weird metaphysical and epistemological paradoxes thrown off by the quantum world would get sorted out and science would settle down with a clean and reducing theory of elementary particles propelled by forceful causes. It is no surprise that Niels Bohr's choice of the ying/yang symbol as the design for his coat of arms for Denmark's highest decoration was met with… raised eyebrows. Even decades later, few writers of fiction (exceptions include American John Barth and Colombian Jorge Luis Borges) dared address the philosophical implications of quantum experiments (see Egginton's sparkling *The Rigor of Angels* (2023) for parallels between Kant, Heisenberg, and Borges).

Meanwhile, as we will see, back at the ivy-covered ranch the modern perspective ensconced at Oxford University 50 years earlier insisted that only the methodology of analytic philosophy qualified as philosophy proper — and Borges and Barth's fictions were definitely not that. Course offerings in Philosophy in Literature (Sartre, Ibsen, Tolstoy) and Philosophical Anthropology (Ernst Cassirer, George Herbert Mead) sparingly sprinkled across American campuses — and taught by securely tenured professors, to be sure — might be delightful. But they were definitely not real philosophy. Not metaphysics; not metaethics. To paraphrase Kant's comment about metaethics over a century earlier, bringing context into professional philosophy would just turn metaphysics into sociology. God forbid.

There was no room for context-dependence in the guild. And therefore no room for mereology (parts–wholes relationships).

The entrenchment of the Newtonian paradigm within the halls of Anglo-American academic philosophy is lamentable, but should not have been surprising. Considering other alternatives would indeed have meant bringing into the heart of metaphysics context-dependent features like *recursion, organization,* and *timing*. It would have meant overthrowing the ruling paradigm's essentialist and atomistic presuppositions on which all of philosophical ontology rested: that reality was particulate and the properties and powers of those independent thing-like elements essential, universal, and unchanging. That Newtonian spacetime was an empty container which did not influence the fundamental properties of its contents. That in consequence, any background context in which entities and processes are embedded is itself likewise universal and featureless. Experimental observation therefore does not leak into the observed.

In short, recognizing the reality of synergies, mutualisms, and interdependencies would have required questioning the received theory's reliance on only one form of causality (linear, not recursive, efficient cause) and a particular understanding of spacetime (as empty, featureless container). It would have required allowing other types of "cause–effect" relations in addition to the *efficient causes* (that transfer energy in billiard-ball fashion) that still dominate the models and theories of contemporary physics. The associated philosophical worldview at the time made any such metaphysical and epistemological alternatives inconceivable.

Accurate predictions and industrial and economic successes attest to the brilliance of Newtonian science, especially as harnessed during the Industrial Revolution along with the second law of thermodynamics. The stunning achievements of modern science are undeniable. This essay in no way questions that. In hindsight, however, it is clear that it also left the West with a worldview that in other respects had serious flaws.

Specifically:

1. The Newtonian-positivist worldview could not account for the progressive and qualitatively novel *complexification* of the universe since the Big Bang—from quantum plasma to complex dynamics such as the Earth's biosphere, not to mention the origin of the human mind and social organization.
2. The standard ontological worldview insisted that systemic qualities are just *epiphenomenal* froth sitting on

top of essential atomistic reality. Consequently, it failed to explain how integrated and coherent wholes arise. This failure applies as well to accounting for those collective dynamics we call families, social organizations, and cultures, whose interdependent constraints undeniably loop back down to influence individuals caught up in their dynamics: families, cultures, and other forms of organization confer dimensions of identity—gender, race, socioeconomic class, culture—all of which have palpable effects on their members. The bottom-up and top-down lines of influence that characterize these complex dynamics were invisible to the dominant Newtonian-infused paradigm. Simply because of its refusal to countenance mereological relations.

3. Neither could the Newtonian and positivist conceptual frameworks account for *axiology*—the domain of *values, from aesthetic to moral*. They cannot because (to come full circle) they lack the conceptual instruments to explain—at any scale—the etiology whereby coherent wholes come into being. The thesis that normativity in general and moral values in particular are merely subjective emotional outbursts or subtle power plays was positivism's sole response our most pressing questions: "What is valuable?" What is *worthy* of being valued, that is. What *is* worth?

The common thread running through these three issues is that the received scientific and philosophical worldview cannot explain *how active lines of influence and constraint weave relations between individuals into integrative totalities characterized by interdependent and emergent properties*. It cannot account for emergent properties because its conceptual framework cannot handle *mereological*—parts–wholes—relations. How do constrained relations between independent entities generate overarching dynamics that we know as social organizations such as families or tribes, beehives and ecosystems? How do constrained relations between individual water molecules—*in* a particular location, *under* particular environmental conditions—generate the overarching dynamics of a whirlpool, or a Bénard cell? In turn, how does each form of coordination and integration (read "each system") influence its constituents (read "members" or "components")—all the while being influenced by them? How does activity at each stage or level of coordination and synergy modify and shape the goings-on at other dimensions of coordination and synergy so that individual components continuously co-vary, co-adjust, and co-evolve to preserve the metastability of the overarching dynamic—while maintaining their individuality?

Ripples from this theoretical cliff reach deep into our lives even today. The disenchantment of the world Max Weber bemoaned is a direct consequence of the intractability of this impasse. We will see that it can be directly traced back to the zeitgeist consolidated by positivism, the most influential school of philosophy since the beginning of the twentieth century. Those ripples reach not only into the way we frame debates about identity and individuation; critically, as just noted, they reach to the roots of our ideas of family, organization, and institution. They have devastated our understanding of community and values—all because of an uncritically accepted principle that interactions with context and parts–wholes relations are merely powerless froth atop reality's particulate core. As a result of this fundamental metaphysical presupposition, we are taught to believe that most of the reality we deal with in our everyday lives is nothing but an epistemic construct.

This monograph will argue that, in the abiotic realm as well as the domain of living things, complex systems are real *patterns* of interdependent matter, energy, and information flow with emergent properties. The most noteworthy features of each emergent dynamic are *sui generis*, qualitatively new powers and capabilities that arise simultaneously with each achieved integrated synergy and mutualism. The category of "complex systems far from equilibrium" spans whirlpools, laser beams, and superfluidity, galaxies, and biospheres (which integrate both abiotic and biotic realms into a coordinated metastable pattern that itself persists far from equilibrium). And, of course, all living things.

But none of this fits in with the received worldview of Newtonian physics in the early part of the twentieth century, especially in combination with the classical version of near equilibrium thermodynamics as the inexorable tendency of energy to become increasingly and homogeneously distributed until the universe reaches a final state of thermal equilibrium (heat death) devoid of energetic potential. White noise. So how to explain a common occurrence: the emergence throughout the universe of pockets of increasingly complex dynamics, each of which locally and temporarily renews cosmic potential with added degrees of freedom. How to explain self-organization by constraints such that the second law is locally and temporarily delayed even as entropy increases overall. The universe seems to display a universal tendency to synthesis. Physics itself is now pondering the Webb telescope's discovery of well-organized galaxies even in the very early universe. The Appendix will describe the path forward, one that borrows from complexity theory to rethink a comprehensive metaphysics of causation in terms of a relational, processual ontology.

**

Once entrenched, however, the Newtonian and positivist framework left in its wake dashed hopes of a metaphysics and epistemology that, by giving processes and constraints their due, might have recognized that "context changes everything." And there things stood for most of the last 125 years. All because philosophers and scientists stuck stubbornly to these apparently *modern* presuppositions, especially with respect to the workings of causes and effects on the one hand and synergetic *interactions among individual entities and with context* on the other. As a result, for pretty much all of the twentieth century and even to date, interdependencies and mutualisms with the embedding context —the environment, milieu, umwelt, niche, habitat, call it what you may—went unseen, ignored, or dismissed by professional philosophers in the Anglo-American academy.

Ignored, that is, except by four women who tried to bring "philosophy back to life;" who attempted, in effect, to bring the full context of a lived life back into professional philosophy. The story of Elizabeth Anscombe, Philippa Foot, Iris Murdoch, and Mary Midgley at Oxford University 1939–1942 will provide the second case study for this monograph. Their private and professional lives are beautifully recounted in three recent and critically acclaimed books: *Metaphysical Animals: How Four Women Brought Philosophy back to Life*; *The Women are Up to Something*; and *A Terribly Serious Adventure*. First as students in the early years of World War 2 and then intermittently as tutors and fellows after the war, the four women struggled

> [t]o bring philosophy back to life, back to the context of the messy everyday reality of a human life lived with

others. Back to the deep connection that ancient philosophers saw between Human Life, Goodness, and Form. Back to the fact that we are living organisms, whose nature and habitat shapes the way we get on and flourish or wither in the world. (Mac Cumhaill and Wiseman 2022—henceforth M&W)

These four so-called "metaphysicals" were concerned not only with what makes for a life well-lived; they reflected on how the actual natural and social environments in which they went about their daily lives contributed to, afforded, stymied, and in general biased conditions towards a life well (or poorly) lived. Phrased in the professional language of the era, the women understood that the fact–value distinction, first formulated by Hume and later consolidated by positivism, was untenable. Empirical facts about the overall context leak into the lives of human beings embedded in that context. Systemic facts of the matter do indeed alter the likelihood that individuals will or will not act in certain ways. Even more importantly, by stacking the deck towards certain consequences for those lives, those facts contribute to the positive or negative valence of the lives of the individuals in question—they have empirically detectable consequences for good or ill. Specifically, for strongly influencing *conditions* for human flourishing. They proposed, in other words, that empirical facts are built into normativity.

However, at the time and often to this day in the Anglo-American academy, fact and value are philosophically assumed to be non-overlapping domains—with each other and with the enveloping world.

This principle was put into doubt by the careful philosophical deliberations of four Englishwomen who showed unequivocally that empirical conditions and value are inextricably intertwined. Context might not determine behavior 1:1 as Newtonian collisions allegedly did, but it is undoubtedly a strong influence. How does *causality-by-overarching-context* work? How do wholes influence parts? Especially such that this "causal mechanism" brings about consequences with novel (in this case axiological) properties? Alas, the philosophical establishment of the day dismissed these four women as *metaphysicals* precisely because positivist philosophy had no room for mereological relations, much less for the idea of localized context-dependent causation.

In Part II of this monograph we will examine the philosophical reflections of these four philosophers who, according to one of their male colleagues, were "*up to something.*" Indeed, they were *on to* something. Our metaphysical women were trying to bring philosophy… back to all the interlocking interdependencies between human beings and the natural and symbolic worlds in which we are immersed and to which we belong. *Belonging* —not just *being plunked into*—is a relation vastly different from that of atoms in the empty and featureless vessel of Newtonian space and time. *Belongingness* and *embeddedness* imply that individual and spatiotemporal context are intertwined and interdependent. That they are aspects of a more encompassing whole. The women tried to bring philosophy back to life *as it is lived* by real people in real conditions. Back to the normativity and values that arise from those interdependencies—back to bringing Wittgenstein's *forms of life* fully into academic philosophical deliberations on ontology and epistemology. These four very good friends understood that only by taking seriously the rich and multidimensional tapestry of a full human life can interlocking and intertwining empirical facts with moral value be made tractable. Only then can some understanding of a well-lived life be formulated. Professionally, their work set the stage for subsequent movements in philosophy: virtue ethics, environmental ethics, and a reconceptualization of agency and human action we now call the 4E approach.

The four changed the direction of philosophy for decades to come.

By detailing their arguments against the positivist worldview, the last section recounts how the four women simultaneously struggled against—but also embodied, embedded, extended, and enacted—the history of twentieth-century British philosophy. The received understanding of cause–effect relations bequeathed by positivism and entrenched in Anglo-American academic circles (especially its dismissal of mereological causes and effects and its understanding of intentional causation) proved too entrenched to allow the four metaphysicals to formulate a novel and synthetic account of the interdependence of fact and value.

It would take almost one hundred years for the North Atlantic Academy to even begin to address the problem. Explaining why is the task of this monograph.

Part I

Chapter 1

The Backstory

The Introduction presented a brief summary of what might be called Anglo-American academic philosophy's bottom-up atomic essentialism: it excludes *mereology* from ontology and epistemology; it excludes, that is, *causal* relations between parts and wholes.

By *wholes* I will mean novel mutualisms and interdependencies that arise in response to constraints. Paradigmatic examples include *organized* units like molecules, cells, tissues, organisms, ecosystems—but also nonliving waves and fields, whirlpools and autocatalytic reactions—each defined by qualitatively novel properties that exist only at the systemic level. Ocean (and stadium!) waves endure *as waves* as they propagate, even though their individual components (water molecules and sports fans) also simultaneously persist and change in time. Cells are differentiated and articulated coherent units held together by constraints that modulate and control their now interdependent but not fused components. This modulation ensures the continued existence of the overarching system-wide dynamic—the sustenance and persistence of the qualitatively novel properties that characterize a cell's overarching dynamic, far from equilibrium—its integral wholeness and novel powers.

Complex dynamical *wholes* are therefore not clumps, lumps, or aggregates; they are not block-like, stuck-together masses. Mitochondria within cells retained many of their own characteristics even as they integrated into the unified whole we call a cell—and even as those mitochondrial features suddenly became regulated/modulated by the cellular matrix in which they are embedded. Unlike slabs of terrazzo flooring, in other words, complex systems *form* and *hang together as coordinated self-stable units*—they become and remain metastable despite being far from thermal equilibrium. Such complex dynamical systems are clearly not additional things or stuff; they are best conceptualized as coordinated, resonating, synchronized *patterns* of matter and energy flow in space and time that endure in dynamic metastability *far from equilibrium*. The novel and defining properties that arise with each new level of coordination and integration emerge with the new interdependencies we observe as patterns.

Finally, those novel qualities are not, as Newtonian mechanics would have it, just cast-off by-products of massed *stuff* pushed around by energetic *forces*. Significantly for purposes of this monograph, they are *not epiphenomenal*: their emergent causative powers do indeed "change the go" of the components. Cells are alive; their organelles, arguably, are not. It is a central tenet of this monograph that complex systems can even alter the very context from which they emerged. Co-evolution is a process of interdependent adaptation and transformation. Naturalizing strong emergence in this way is a central feature of the new science of complexity.

In all fairness, in the first decades of the twentieth century there was simply no naturalistic terminology with which to articulate a countervailing thesis that the cosmos in general, including the emergence of life, human cognition, and moral values, might be better understood in terms of a tendency (impetus? conatus?) to synthesize and sustain *coherent and persistent dynamic patterns of mass, energy, and information.* Much less to hypothesize that the generation and persistence of those dynamics might involve a form of "cause" — namely constraints — that operates other than as transfers of energy as envisioned by "efficient cause." The very intelligibility of such a conceptual reorganization awaited not only the development of nonlinear, far from equilibrium dynamical systems theory during the last third of the century; it awaited its acceptance and widespread influence. Accepting the new perspective took a while; the proverbial paradigm shift did not gather momentum until the first quarter of the twenty-first century. At the time, for those committed to a more natural realism, reduction to elementary particles pushed around by forceful causes was the only available metaphysical option; its hope was that a scientifically informed Philosophy of Everything might account for strongly emergent properties.

This conviction played out in odd ways. For example, Henri Bergson's *élan-vital*-based emergentism (*Creative Evolution*, 1907) postulated an *immanent* and creative life force that activates matter from within and can therefore account for top-down causation — *from* a causally potent living thing as a whole *to* its behavior and components. But by the first half of the twentieth century the notion of a *vital impetus* just could not rid itself of a whiff of dualism; Bergsonian emergentism was taken to postulate some sort of old-fashioned matter on the one hand pushed about by spooky spiritual forces on the other (see Juarrero and Rubino 2010).

This misunderstanding over the exact causal mechanism whereby *élan vital* activates matter did not ameliorate the general philosophical neglect of the lived context and the past — indeed it simply ensured the active dismissal of these two from ontology and epistemology, an approach shaped a general mindset that has since permeated Western popular culture in practically every realm. It encapsulates a perspective that systematically neglects the dynamic context and the past.

But the tendency to dismiss spatiotemporal context began much earlier. A number of academic milestones in the late nineteenth century and early twentieth century had steadily begun to nudge German and British idealism off center stage as the dominant philosophical worldview of European and U.S. intellectual life. Specifically, the appeal of Hegel's Absolute Being and its manifestation in the material world had already started to unravel thanks to the spreading influence of Kant's earlier *critical* idealism and its *epistemological turn* (of which more below).

Idealism Fades Away

To bring to light this quintessentially Anglo-American Backstory, two distinct if intertwined epistemological trajectories need to be tracked simultaneously: one about *knowledge of the external world*, the other about *knowledge of values, including moral values*. Both record Hegel's and Kant's diminishing influence in the U.S. and the U.K. by the end of the nineteenth century—specifically, their theses of reality as objective Absolute Being in the case of Hegel and of the reality of moral freedom and agency in the case of Kant. The two threads shared a growing mistrust in "self-transcending illumination" and "moral intuitionism" as a mode of either acquiring knowledge of the empirical world on the one hand or of apprehending moral qualities on the other. The latter track took longer to crumble thanks to British realists G.E. Moore and H.M. Prichard's proposal that (unlike facts about the empirical world) *moral qualities can* be directly grasped by a distinctly human faculty of moral intuition. For moral intuitionists like Moore and Prichard, a version of perception could be trusted to acquire knowledge of moral values.

At the time I wrote "Does Action Theory Rest on a Mistake?" (Juarrero-Roque 1985), I did not fully appreciate that these two trajectories come together precisely at the intersection of the generalized goal-directedness of living things on the one hand, and human purposive action on the other. Specifically, I did not associate the failures of mid-twentieth-century philosophical action theory with Kant's remarks about teleology in the *Critique of Judgment* to the effect that, unlike our understanding of causal relations in the nonliving world, the intrinsic goal-directedness that guides and sustains living things involves *recursive and iterative influences*.

Critically (Juarrero-Roque 1985), Kant equated *purposiveness* with *self-organization* and self-organization with recursion. He noted, for example, that trees produce leaves but are in turn produced by their leaves. But that observation contradicted Western philosophy's ban on circular causality—a prohibition as old as Aristotle (*Metaphysics IX*)—a ban that Hume reaffirmed in light of Newton's understanding of linear causal relations. In light of this insistence on linear causal relations, Western scientists and philosophers never entertained the hypothesis that recursive mereological relations might generate coherent forms. While idealism was still the rage, one could only infer that coherence must be given *a priori*. As a result, Kant concluded that the interactions between trees and their leaves thus embody a "form of causality unknown to us"—such relations therefore do not constitute the phenomenal world. My main point: because of the prohibition against mereological relations, Kant in effect threw out the baby of natural self-organization with the perceived bathwater of classical teleology.

Scientist-philosopher Michael Polanyi might have come closest to a revival of Kantian purposiveness as self-organization. In the end, however, the Hungarian-British thinker balked at accepting that boundary conditions of complex systems might themselves self-organize. The possibility that the primordial organizational framework is not imposed—cosmically, by God—but can bootstrap itself from the very dynamics of natural but recursive processes like feedback and autocatalysis was never considered (Juarrero 2013). Upshot: Polanyi too ended up dismissed by Anglo-American positivists as a polymath "continental philosopher." *Personal Knowledge* (1946), Polanyi's seminal critique of positivism, suffered the same fate as von Bertalanffy systems theory and, as we shall see below, Köhler's gestalts. The same fate as Whitehead's idea of *concrescence* as a form of causal relations between entities.

Polanyi was just following tradition. Kant's refusal to countenance recursivity in parts–wholes relations was never disavowed by philosophers generally, and not only in the Anglo-American world. In *Metaphysics IX* Aristotle had ruled out any role for circular causation in metaphysics; in light of Newton's influence, twentieth-century philosophers were not about to revive it. Consequently, Western philosophy never accepted that mereological and recursive interactions between, say, a living thing and its components might constitute a natural form of self-organization. The refusal to acknowledge circular causality has remained firmly in place in the history of Western philosophy generally. The possibility that restricting causal relations to efficient causes might have something to do with our inability to make goal-directedness tractable was never addressed. Few thinkers paid any mind to recursive processes and self-organization—except, in retrospect, for logician-mathematicians Kurt Gödel and Alan Turing. Only after the reintroduction of recursive algorithms in computer science did the issue resurface.

The recalcitrance concerning recursive causation continues firmly entrenched in academic metaphysics to this day—if in a different guise: it appears primarily in deliberations on the "mind-body problem." If, as Aristotle, Newton, and Hume maintained, *recursive causation is* metaphysically impossible as a source of emergent properties, then neither can emergent self-organized brain dynamics nor purposive behavior in general and human intentional causes in particular be the natural outcome of *feedback loops* of socially embedded, enacted, embodied, and extended neuronal networks organized within a particular (social) context. A naturalized understanding of agency and purposive behavior also becomes impossible, and for the same reason (Juarrero 1999).

Thus did the trajectory of philosophy take an egregiously wrong turn for the next two hundred years.

> **MEREOLOGICAL RELATIONS: THE FIRST FORK NOT TAKEN**
>
> Neither Kant *nor scientists or philosophers after him explored new ways of conceptualizing causes and effects.* Instead, as we will see below, thanks to a combination of a revival of realism and the successes of Newtonian mechanics, efficient causality became entrenched as the sole form of causality allowed. The empirical world henceforth had to be thought of as operating exclusively in terms of forceful collisions.

The following chapter briefly summarizes the backdrop that precipitated Kant's "epistemological turn." Those familiar with the philosophy of idealism can skip ahead.

Chapter 2

Track 1
Knowledge of the External World

Modern Idealism vs. Modern Realism

Hegel's nineteenth-century version of *idealism* had contended that human reason is isomorphic with the Absolute. One consequence of this view is that Absolute Being, the ground of all reality, renders itself knowable to the human mind in a sort of illumination of self-awareness. According to idealism, perceptions contain nothing that is not in the essence of reality; conversely, in the essence of reality there is nothing that is not manifested in perception. British idealists of the period such as F.H. Bradley and T.H. Green concurred. Although some thinkers in the United States like Emerson and Thoreau were more disposed to think of idealism as a form of spiritualism (which they contrasted with materialism), mainstream objective idealists like Josiah Royce at Harvard subscribed to the standard understanding of idealism that held that the human mind can come to know objective and rational reality because it is somehow One with it. This literal identity between mind and Being makes *what* human beings experience of the world One with their subjective experience *of it.*

So far, so straightforward idealism, whether Hegel's Absolute Idealism or American versions of it, Royce's American idealism and Emerson and Thoreau's transcendentalism.

KANT'S "CATEGORIES" REPLACE IDEALIST "ILLUMINATION"

Kant's transcendental Categories of the Understanding replace Hegel's illuminating epiphanies of Becoming and Being as the source of knowledge of the empirical world. By cognitively structuring—*a priori*—our perceptions, the Categories demarcate what human beings can know about the phenomenal realm.

That said, twenty-five years or so before Hegel published *Phenomenology of Spirit* in 1807, the philosopher from Königsberg, Immanuel Kant, had published a general critique of idealism. *Critical* idealism, the modified idealism for which Kant is best known and which marked the beginning of the "epistemological" or "critical" turn in Western philosophy, set limits to empirical knowledge. Kant argued that *noumena*, the empirical world as it is in itself (*an sich*), cannot be accessed directly, even in illuminating epiphanies as Idealists claimed. We cannot know *noumena* because our cognition cannot bypass *a priori* filters that transcendental *Categories of the Understanding* build into the mind. We can only know *phenomena*, the external world *as it appears to us*—that is, as filtered through (structured by) *the Categories*.

One of these Kantian categories is causality. Human beings must experience phenomena in terms of causal categories; phrased otherwise, the unitary human subject necessarily organizes perceptions sequentially as causes and effects. Phenomenon 1 can be determined to constitutively cause phenomenon 2 when two perceptions are ordered as a necessary sequence. Kant's critical idealism maintained that the necessary connection is itself not directly sensed; it is given by the Category of causality's *a priori* structuring of the human mind. (For readers familiar with this history, Kant's *a priori* Category of causality purportedly provided the "necessary connection" between the two impressions that Hume's sensory apparatus failed to detect.) In other words, phenomena can be determined to be objectively related *as* cause and effect when human subjects must perceive them as a necessary *connection* between *impression 1* and a subsequent, closely contiguous *impression 2*, with which it is *regularly correlated*. The necessity correlation warrants our belief that such impressions constitute real experience. Today we might rephrase this by saying that selection pressures provide a necessary filter between a human subject's perceptions and the real world. (More on the mischief wrought by optical illusions and hallucinations later.)

The Dismissal of the Superego from Academic Philosophy—Sigmund Freud

Almost a century after Kant, echoes of his Categories are present in Sigmund Freud's revolutionary ideas about a hypothesized "subconscious" mental realm. Readers will recall that Freud proposed that a *culture's social expectations* are central to the formation of the *superego*, which develops through the conscious and unconscious integration of the *id*'s demands—as reframed in a culturally acceptable manner. In this interpretation, culture serves as an embedding context (or a quasi-category of social understanding, as it were—today's concept of "framing") that shapes and governs the *a priori-given framework* that structures the superego.

Neither Freud's relations linking individuals to culture nor Kant's intertwining a subject's perceptual sequences into a coherent unit were said to be directly *sensed*. There simply is no causal mechanism in Newtonian physics that philosophers of science at the time could use to understand mereological influences *from* wholes like "cultures" *to* their components or members. Even if it were acknowledged that individuals can become embedded in, intertwined with each other and their environment, Newtonian-informed epistemology tells us that the mind can only be epiphenomenal and instrumental froth—icing with no power of its own to bring about anything. As such, and even if they parallel hydraulic processes, mental processes as such are subjective and ineffective. Since, like Marx but unlike Kant, Freud purported to be doing *empirical science*, not idealist philosophy, his very idea of "culture" ended up being judged a mental construct as well. No part of ontology because no way to account for its etiology.

It is therefore unsurprising that by the beginning of the twentieth century, philosophers in the Anglophone world (who were by then already dubious of Kant's *a priori* transcendental categories) came to consider Freudian speculation about socially-constructed mental frames to be as unverifiable and unscientific as Kant's. Or Jung's, for that matter. By postulating a new and even more mysterious mental realm beyond regular awareness, Freud's "unconscious" was even worse than transcendental categories: neither unconscious mental categories nor superegos remotely qualified as legitimate "causal" powers—because top-down powers from whole to parts are no "form of causality" known to philosophy. Seeming wholes did not even qualify as real integral unities—ontologically they are mere clumped aggregates reducible to the sum of their components. Hence Kant's refusal to countenance recursive causality brought about an "epistemological" turn that put ontology forevermore in doubt.

As the proponent of a new philosophical psychology, Freud found a receptive audience in universities on the European continent—as did Marx. But since mereological relations (especially top-down, *from* whole *to* parts) are not part of the "furniture of the world"—because wholes are not—Anglo-American philosophy departments judged Freud's hypotheses about influences *from* an embedding context (cultural, subconscious superego, or otherwise) *on* individuals immersed in that context as *not metaphysics* because they are incompatible with the standard understanding of causal relations enshrined in Newtonian mechanics. Especially in the United States, Freud's ideas about nested layers of cognitive and affective mental organization—and their relation to society—were turned over to university psychology departments (the first one of which had recently been organized for William James at Harvard—whose ideas, incidentally, and for analogous reasons, did not belong in philosophy departments. See below.) Other disciplines claiming to be scientific—economics, sociology, and even biology—were treated similarly; they too were disqualified as "science" because practitioners in those fields could not formulate deterministic laws like Newton's laws of motion operating through efficient causes impacting fundamental particles.

Slowly, interest in Kantian Categories, initially postulated as saviors of the appearances, began to fade. British and American philosophers steadily reoriented towards more contemporary versions of empiricism and realism. In the wake of the successes of Newtonian science, the Academy turned towards a more Humean stance, towards an emphasis on *natural law*—that is, to universal and deterministic "constant conjunctions" that support counterfactuals. Perceptual invariances and covariances required the discovery of deterministic natural laws to underpin the counterfactuals the invariances revealed.

The next sections explain the reasoning behind *this* revamped philosophical edifice.

Analytic Philosophy and the Vienna Circle

During the first decades of the twentieth century, the city of Vienna "turned the world modern" (Cockett 2023). Along with Impressionist painters and designers of Art Nouveau and Art Deco, Freud today is recognized as having contributed to this movement. But as just mentioned, philosophy at the time, especially in the Anglo-American world, looked primarily to physics, mathematics, and symbolic logic for inspiration; as a result, the most influential of the era's conceptual innovations was a scientifically and mathematically-informed approach to philosophy. Of the philosophical schools that arose during those years, the one with the longest reach originated among members of the so-called Vienna Circle, an exclusive group of scientifically oriented philosophers and intellectuals who met regularly in that city with the aim of formulating "a scientific conception of the world." It was called positivism.

The central thesis of the Vienna Circle was that statements about the empirical world, formulated in declarative sentences, must be understood, not by elucidating how Kantian transcendental categories frame human understanding, much less by referencing Hegelian insight and intuition into Absolute Being and Becoming. The meaning of declarative sentences must be gleaned through careful analyses of their logical form. Semantics is revealed in the structure of contentless, meaningless syntax.

To anchor their theories, Circle members first turned to German philosopher Gottlieb Frege's 1879 paper which promised to derive all of mathematics from formal logic. Frege had hoped to show that formal axiomatic systems capture the language of *pure* thought (articulated in well-formed logical formulas unencumbered with semantic content). As an example, selecting and defining the postulates and fundamental operations of axiomatic systems lets us deduce the entire edifice of arithmetic from a foundation in logic. To that end, Frege deployed *set theory*, which is about properties of groups and properties of members of those groups. For example, Frege defined number, n, generally as the "class or set of all collections of n members;" the number 7 in turn is the class or set of all collections of 7 members. Frege even invented fancy new universal ∀ and existential ∃ quantifiers for the operations of predicate logic performed on these classes. The Vienna Circle enthusiastically adopted a notion of truth and inference using Frege's existential and universal quantifiers.

Frege's innovations thereby paved the way for the *logical picture theory of language.*

(It is worth adding at this point that Frege also believed that, by stripping semantics from logical propositions, which in turn stripped them of empirical meaning and reference, the resulting elaboration of Boolean algebra simultaneously removed from philosophy the need for *intuition* of any sort. In light of the non-Euclidean geometries of Nikolav Lobachevsky (1829) and especially Bernhard Riemann (1854, published 1868), both of whom called into question the allegedly indubitable "self-evidence" of the Parallel Postulate of Cartesian geometry, rejecting intuition in any guise was enthusiastically welcomed by the younger philosophers at Oxford and Cambridge. Logical relations came across as much more "modern" than either built-in categories of the mind, Cartesian "clear and distinct ideas," or that mystical faculty, Idealist illumination. Or intuition.)

The Vienna Circle's seminal philosophical work was a text compiled by Ludwig Wittgenstein, a peripheral member of the Circle, from work he had done with Bertrand Russell at Cambridge before the First World War and partially written while Wittgenstein was in the trenches during the war. By expanding on Frege's elaboration of Boolean algebra, Wittgenstein's aphoristic *Tractatus Logico-Philosophicus* (1921, in English in 1922) captured the Vienna Circle's ideas about a "picture theory of language." It proposed that declarative sentences are analogous to logical pictures: their grammar depicts "atomic facts" in such a way that the logical structure of the sentence's syntax faithfully represents the actual structure (the facts) of the world. Syntax gets you semantics.

It is not difficult to appreciate how, in light of the successes of modern physics and advances in formal logic, philosophers at the time were keen to replace idealism with the more modern notion of logical "pictures." The hope was that in so doing a more accurate understanding of reality would emerge. Perhaps Frege's new notation might help. The Vienna Circle's thesis that formal analysis undistorted by commonplace language usage provides the sole standard for determining empirical truth and certifying knowledge about the natural world became known as *logical positivism* and *formal analysis*.

As an example: Russell proposed that even troubling counterfactual sentences like "The present king of France is bald" could be elucidated through formal logical analysis. Once analyzed as Russell suggested, logical analysis could expose the source of certain forms of errors — the error was just hidden behind seemingly meaningful but actually nonsensical sentences. Along the way, formal analysis could also expose deductive arguments in which such nonsensical sentences serve as premises as *unsound*.

Analysis grounded in formal logic promised to debunk many age-old metaphysical claims and controversies with the new tools of Boolean algebra developed by Frege. Along the way, these tools would also undermine other allegedly empirical statements, not just those about imaginary kings of France. In short, Vienna Circle philosophers turned to formal analysis not only because of its novel contributions to theoretical mathematics and logic; its key selling point was Fregean logic's perceived power to expose *metaphysical* statements that *seem to "point to" existing referents*. Fast-forward the through-line: the radical philosophical conclusion promised by formal analysis was that the grammar of metaphysical statements would be revealed as not picturing anything objectively real — it would reveal that, in general, metaphysical talk was in fact nonsensical. The object and allegedly representational content of metaphysics were not even wrong; they were meaningless.

The Vienna Circle's numerous and influential followers in the West quickly subscribed to this approach and Frege-inspired logical positivism soon eclipsed Kant's Categories of the Understanding and Hegelian illumination; it deployed the new quantifiers to break down the very grammar of apparently meaningful sentences in ordinary language. Unveiling a sentence's true logical form unobscured by fuzzy connotations promised to reveal egregious errors; formal logic, that is, could expose that what some sentences seem to be stating is at best misleading. I will return later to the worm lurking in Frege's logic, but suffice to say that at the time and for decades thereafter, the possibility that purely syntactical (meaningless) language might be inadequate to describe the full richness of reality was not even entertained—except by rare outliers like Hans Reichenbach. Until Kurt Gödel's devastating work put an end to any hope that a formal axiomatic system could be both consistent *and complete*, formal logic's inability to deal with paradox—and its disambiguation by context—went unremarked, except by Russell, who had earlier (also in *Principia Mathematica*) tried to make tractable the worm in Frege's logic, as we will see below. Even then, Anglo-American philosophers did not embrace the role of context for either metaphysics or epistemology.

The Vienna Circle's formal approach to language and thought (begun with a reliance on Frege and later consolidated with Russell and Whitehead's *Principia Mathematica*) was the decisive step that nudged Anglo-American philosophy away from both Hegel's Absolute and Kant's critical idealism. Henceforth the direction of North Atlantic philosophy veered in a different direction, towards a deductively justified and observationally confirmed realism. To repeat: no one except perhaps some Romantic poets (Taylor 2024) and existentialists even noticed that this modern perspective came at a price: the total rejection of any role for context in the apprehension, constitution, and disambiguation of meaning and semantics—the dismissal of any role for significance and meaning—for coherence—in other words. Claude Shannon's theory of (just as meaningless) information would share a similar fate forty-some years later.

Meanwhile, here's the rest of the story.

Logical Positivism

Along with *avant garde* innovations in the arts, logical positivism indeed turned philosophy modern. In its attempt to ground all mathematics on principles of logic (which after Frege and even for philosophers came to mean something like Boolean algebra, not just clear thinking to a purpose), logical positivists remade philosophy in the image of theoretical (logico-mathematical) physics; henceforth, *only* logical deduction from fundamental law-like regularities and premises verified by observation would be considered proper philosophical reasoning. So-called hypothetico-deductive inferences became the dominant model of explanation. By relying on formal analysis, logical positivism replaced idealism in holding out the promise of reinstating a fully realist ontology. When combined with the *principle of verification (*to be explained below), *formal analytic philosophy* —and its more informal heir, *ordinary language philosophy*— would enthrall Anglo-American philosophers for the next 75 years.

The World Turns Modern

Between the wars, a number of British philosophers including G.E. Moore, A.J. Ayer, Susan Stebbing, and Willard Van Orman Quine spent time in Austria studying with members of the Vienna Circle. After his return to Oxford from Vienna just before the outbreak of WWII, 24-year-old A.J. (Freddie) Ayer became Britain's most influential advocate of positivism. In his 1936 book *Language, Truth, and Logic*, Ayer explored how best to redirect philosophers towards formal logical analysis—the better to spot concepts that are not empirically verifiable. The better to debunk metaphysics in general.

As sketched above, the unstated hypothesis underpinning formal analysis was that deductive proofs of axiomatic systems can warrant knowledge of the external world. But to offer both a theory of meaning and a theory of truth in addition to a theory of knowledge acquisition, positivism's emphasis on logic had to show that deductive reasoning was not only *valid*; its arguments needed to be *sound*. That is, the syntactically well-formed axioms and initial condition premises on which the deduction rested had to be empirically true as well. Only empirically true statements guarantee claims to *soundness* and thus yield *knowledge of the world*. But if (in addition to logical validity) an argument's soundness depends on the truth of its premises, what guarantees *their* truthfulness? If (even in a Kantian guise) idealism is unscientific because knower and known are different entities and transcendental categories therefore don't warrant any empirical claims to knowing reality in itself—if Descartes is wrong and there exist no clear and distinct perceptions that self-validate foundational axioms—how can axioms about the furniture of the world be certified (verified) *as* empirically true?

The oft-cited concluding line of Wittgenstein's *Tractatus* encapsulates the philosophical spirit of the times: "Whereof one cannot speak [meaningfully, that is, via logical analysis and verified sensory impressions], thereof one must remain silent." If there are no self-validating perceptual impressions from which to build a scientific theory, how far can syntax validate any claim concerning the empirical world?

The Second Fork Not Taken

As evidence that scholars who did not subscribe to the principles of logical positivism were excluded from the curricula of Anglo-American philosophy departments, just consider:

- As mentioned earlier, the writings of Ralph Waldo Emerson and Henry David Thoreau had already been handed off to the literature faculty and disparagingly labeled "transcendentalism:" these essays were, at best, self-help manuals in the spirit of Epictetus's *Enchiridion*. Worse, their reasoning had neither the rigor nor systematicity of either a Kant or Hegel.
- Physiology professor William James understood conscious experience *as not subject alone, but as the integration of subject-plus-object*. But what can underpin such integration given that physics had no concept of causality to account for synthetic processes generally—much less epistemic ones? James's views of consciousness were consequently quickly shunted alongside Freud to the first ever academic department of psychology, a department, incidentally, Harvard created especially for James. In turn, James's ideas on religion ended up in whichever department, theology or religion, would accept them. Just keep them out of philosophy departments.

- In light of positivism's emphasis on Boolean logic, American scientist and mathematician Charles Sanders Peirce's proposals for a new logic he called *abduction* were likewise ignored; Peirce's "pragmatism" was safely sequestered with John Dewey's in schools of education or in a newly created discipline, sociology. (And this despite the fact that, arguably, Peirce's ideas offer a theory of meaning, and James's ideas constitute a theory of truth.)
- Although Danish thinker Søren Kierkegaard is now considered a foundational precursor of existentialism, his emphasis on faith showed him to be more a theologian than a philosopher. Likewise, Friedrich Nietzsche's focus on life-affirmation as the source of meaning in a meaningless world and his key notion of perspectivism (there is no universal truth, therefore), put him at odds with an increasingly influential physics-enamored community of philosophers.
- The prose style of continental philosophers didn't help; indeed, the nonfiction style of Nietzsche and Kierkegaard was just too far from the language of empirical verification and grammatical meaningfulness to offer a "scientific conception of the world." They were just not philosophers. Compared to his works of fiction, Sartre's nonfiction was as impenetrable as Nietzsche's aphorisms. This dismissal from the philosophical canon was confirmed by the Nobel committee's decision, years later, to award French existentialists Jean-Paul Sartre and Albert Camus the prize... in Literature.
- Fast forward to European structuralist philosophers like Emile Durkheim, Claude Levi-Strauss, and Jean Piaget, among others: comparable outcome—they

were viewed in the Anglophone philosophy world as sociologists, anthropologists, ethnologists, and psychologists. But not philosophers.
- To this day, practically the only institutions of higher learning in the United States that ever bothered with *process philosophy* (formulated by English philosopher-mathematician and Russell co-author Alfred North Whitehead and later elaborated by homegrown American philosopher Charles Hartshorne) were the University of Texas and a few Catholic colleges.

The consensus about continental philosophers, in summary, was that although they might have had interesting personalities, they were not philosophers. This was also true of Spaniards José Ortega y Gassett and Miguel de Unamuno. Unamuno's novels and poetry spoke for themselves: they were literature. As will be described in Part II, Iris Murdoch intuited this bias against novelists; she also knew that Oxford philosophy would never be convinced otherwise.

I used to think that the exclusion of many of these thinkers betrayed a Northern European bias against Southern European enthusiasms. I am now increasingly persuaded that a more general "pre-judice" was in play. Sidelining these schools of philosophy was more likely the inevitable consequence of the fact that these mostly European thinkers had tried — each in his own way — to get beyond essentialism and reductionism and bring context back into philosophy. Disparaging Nietzsche as a "cultural critic" provides some evidence of that. Ortega's now prescient *"yo soy yo y mis circunstancias"* (I am I and my circumstances) conceptualized individuals in terms of class membership (the masses vs. the "select"), but he never clearly explained the causal relations between the individual and society as a whole. And since mereology was not to be countenanced, Ortega's writings too were ignored.

So back to the story. As we have seen, formal analysis could be used to certify well-formed syntax, but British and American realists of a positivist bent still needed to justify the empirical veridicality of the premises themselves. This was particularly important for realists for whom, in contrast to idealist claims, recall, started from the premise that what is known (perceived) is distinct from the knower (perceiver). "Knowledge [not just perception] is *discovery*, the finding of what already is... Knowledge and known are two different things" (Krishnan 2023, p. 8—H.A. Prichard). So how to determine the truth of empirical observations/perceptions?

To address this question, *realist* empiricists of the period turned to German philosopher and psychologist Franz Brentano (1884). In contrast to the picture theory of language inspired by Frege, empty grammatical constructions were not Brentano's concern. Instead, he reintroduced the medieval concept of the *intentionality* of consciousness, the *aboutness* that characterizes thoughts, beliefs, and other mental processes. When I think about a particular friend, for example, my mental state is *intentional*: it is *about* (points to?) an entity other than myself. My friend, the object (and content) of my thought, is a concrete individual spatio-temporally distinct from me, the thinking subject. According to Brentano, this feature of consciousness is at the core of any attribution of mentality. The empiricist realists at the beginning of the twentieth century agreed. But how to verify its truth?

The ever-present possibility that imagination and optical illusions might serve up unreal or distorted objects of perception had been obvious to realists for centuries (even Descartes had worried about evil demons and dreams). The resulting challenge for realists was therefore to make sure that *what* is experienced or perceived in fact faithfully mirrors the objective world—and that subjects are not misled into believing it is so when it is not. To reply to these concerns, early twentieth-century realists were forced once again to confront timeworn questions that empiricists like Locke and Hume had struggled with centuries earlier: if knower and known are distinct and pre-existing entities, what is it about the *interaction* between knower and known that certifies the outcome as *knowledge*—such that subjects come to *know* empirical facts about the world—that A is C, say? How can we *know* anything outside ourselves to be true? Idealists thought the interaction occurred in the form of an illumination; Descartes argued that it was by starting with "clear and distinct" ideas; Kant claimed synthetic *a priori* truths were apprehended in terms of a human subject's mental framework as structured by the categories of the understanding; logical positivists proposed that the syntactical structure of sentences pictured the world.

Twentieth-century realists argued that precise empirical observation should supplement logical analysis.

Realism: Knowledge Acquisition as the Outcome of Sensory Collisions with the External World

In other words, to ensure empirical conclusions and predictions are true, knowledge claims had to be verified by establishing the faithful *transmission* of information about/from the world to the knower's sensory and cognitive apparatus. Perceptions could guarantee true propositions and predictions only if rigorously verified. However, in light of the distorting potential of optical illusions, Cartesian evil genies, dream states, and the like, even simple (and unaltered and uninterpreted) sensory impressions demanded verification. Realists needed to guarantee the uninterrupted faithfulness of transmission—*from* an object distinct from the perceiver on the one hand *to* the perceiver on the other. Verification here also meant that absent any transcendental and inbuilt Kantian Categories, the perceiver's role was to be a faithful, passive, and transparent "mirror of nature" (Rorty). Not identical with an idealist One, just its faithful mirror.

By the beginning of the twentieth century, however, there was no unseeing Newton.

To qualify as a science-informed philosophy, therefore, the *transmission* of information *from* the world *to* the perceiver could only be conceived along the lines of *mechanical causes*: successful and veridical perception must be the product of *collisions* between two separate and distinct bodies—A, in *the outside world*, on B, *the subject's senses* (and I do mean bodies, localizable physical stuff). At a minimum, the manner in which efficient causation operates required "that A and B should be different from one another" (Krishnan 2023, p. 8; Juarrero 1999, 2023). That much conformed with the principles of realism: so far so good. Next, Newtonian interactions between the two must take the form of "collisions" between the senses and the objective world; efficient causes must underpin the transference of information *from* the world (object known) *to* the "detecting mechanism" (human sensory apparatus? experimental apparatus?).

Faithful efficient causes were thus held to underwrite not only actual causal power transfer between objects; they also underwrote the veridicality of the *relation* between the object of perception and the empirical experience itself. (See part II on Anscombe and "wayward causal chains.") Imparting information from the "object" known to the knower's primary sensory impressions can only occur as forceful collisions of *particulate elements*: perceived phenomena are the effects of energy transfer from one to another. Incidentally, this is still the way the puzzles of Bell's inequality and quantum entanglement are conceptualized to this day. Might this conceptualization be at the heart of those puzzles?

SECOND FORK NOT TAKEN: SENSE IMPRESSIONS ARE NOT OF HOLISTIC SCENES

The universality of Newton's laws of motion combined with the mathematization of logic reinforced the belief that knowledge of the external world was possible—but only if empirically verified. The exclusive emphasis on efficient causality, however, favored a bumper car model of causal relations between knower and known: the external world impacts the subject to produce sense impressions. As discussed at length in *Context Changes Everything*, the unnoticed but ubiquitous commitment to mechanical cause–effect relations unavoidably committed early twentieth-century realism to the conclusion that coherent dynamics itself must be powerless and epiphenomenal. This conclusion plays out in the inevitable devolution of "verification of experiential data" to pointillistic "sense data."

The Verification Principle

Logical positivism's understanding of verification echoed that of the empiricists of earlier centuries, with a twist. It must be admitted that Hume did not provide clear criteria for differentiating simple impressions from simple ideas;

but, significantly, neither did he seem to doubt that *the force and vivacity of simple impressions faithfully mirror coherent and constant objects really out there like balls and windowpanes*. In contrast with such earlier empiricists, positivism's verification principle went much farther: it required that verifiable simple sensory impressions be much more granular—only pointillistic and therefore uninterpreted data are acceptable as fully truthful.

Sense Data

In other words, in consequence of its continuing dismissal of recursion and iteration as possible mechanisms of real integration and control, positivism prioritized radical atomism in the epistemological domain as well. In *Language, Truth, and Logic*, Ayer supplemented the Vienna Circle's emphasis on formal logic by insisting that for sense impressions to warrant knowledge acquisition they had to be much more fine-grained than Hume's simple impressions. It was not coincidental, of course, that insisting that only epistemic atomism can verify empirical truth claims echoed Russell's *logical atomism* as articulated in *Principia Mathematica*. Russell and Whitehead's efforts to ground mathematics on symbolic logic had offered a logical picture theory that demanded supplementation by atomistic micro sensory impressions. Logical positivism's verification principle satisfied this requirement: only particulate sensory data can verify empirical experience, because the world and sense perception make direct contact only at the finest—read microgranular—level. These came to be known as *sense data*.

In conformity with Russell's logical atomism, that is, the verification principle insisted on *atomistic sensory data*. The issue was truth, not Impressionism's aesthetics. Because only *microsensory impressions* verify atomic facts, logical positivists concluded that what I see before me is not a fulsome tomato in my hand, much less a "*ripe red* tomato;" my empirically verifiable perception is only of a small patch of vivid red in my visual field. Specific textures, odors, tactile experiences, etc. systematically accompany the sensation of redness, but are independent of each other, according to logical positivism; the perception that *There is a tomato in my hand* goes beyond a simple sensory impression; we do not directly perceive ripeness itself. Even such a minimalist scene of a ripe tomato in my hand might be a fallible construct of our minds and thus impossible to distinguish from optical illusions and hallucination. *Mutatis mutandis,* the same applies to auditory and tactile sensations: we hear only a high-pitched warbling sound, we do not hear an ambulance siren; we experience salty flavor and a crunchy sensation, we do not taste a potato chip itself.

Atomist ontologies with room only for efficient causes operating on essential properties had already demoted apparent unities to epiphenomenal froth. As Artigiani (2021) notes, the revolution brought about by Pointillist and Impressionist artists had also set the stage for a parallel modern stance about knowledge acquisition: what we actually see on a canvas are only tiny dabs of unmixed color. That much is indubitable and truthful. The idea that individual mental processes might themselves be capable of interlocking into covarying (because veridical) perceptual *gestalts* with emergent properties such as ripeness was not within the framework of logical positivism. The overall scene we perceive might also be an epistemic construct our minds assemble from those particulate sense impressions.

Only the most atomistic and pointillistic sensations can warrant truth because only particulate sensations are reliably veridical—strictly speaking, in other words, the *senses never directly perceive coherent wholes out there* because coherence cannot be directly and infallibly sensed—not least because there is no Kantian category of the understanding that structures those sense impressions. Sensed *wholes* (like a red tomato) that even Hume had allowed to qualify as basic impressions were now demoted to a role analogous to the part complex *ideas* played in Locke and Hume: they were constructs. In contrast with Hume's primary sense *impressions,* we have no direct warrant of complex scenes. They are never directly sensed; they are cognitively constructed.

Atomism insisted that only the particulate is real. Sense data theory and the verification principle now offered a parallel approach in epistemology. As an unintended consequence of atomism, requiring radically granular empirical verification effectively also barred from the domain of *both* metaphysics and epistemology the very ideas of coordination, synchrony, alignment, attunement, timing, or any other such type of interdependencies. It barred any form of integrative wholeness from reality and cognition. *Perceptual coherence is at best* an epiphenomenal epistemic construct. The verifiability principle's emphasis on sense data was just what the doctor ordered.

The historical upshot? The Vienna Circle needed a verification principle to support its empirically realist stance; the truth of observations serving as premises in deductive proofs had to be *verified*. Oxford philosopher A.J. Ayer's proposal of a positivist *verification principle* quickly became not just a method but the dominant philosophical dogma of the next several decades: only empirically verifiable propositional statements are meaningful. Only meaningful propositions can be truth-bearing. *And, most critical of all, verification must be grounded on sense data.* Centuries earlier,

Descartes had speculated that an evil genie might trick us into thinking we are awake when we are dreaming. Centuries after Descartes, Kant had proposed that *a priori* Categories of the Understanding frame the way we constitute the world and thereby certify the sense-making links among our perceptions. Telescopes, microscopes, and other instruments of the natural sciences had long been known to make the objects observed smaller and larger — improving the *resolution* of those instruments meant being able to see two stars, galaxies, or organelles and cells *as separate entities*. But pointedly, telescopes and microscopes do not directly detect coordination, timing, tuning, and the rest of the interlocking synergies that comprise wholeness, either epistemically or ontologically. So for critics of positivism and the verification principle, the question suddenly became: How does Humpty — whether in the guise of the fulsome red tomato I see before me, or a living organism implementing homeostasis — get back together again (from the shards of atomistic sense data and component parts)?

At this point "All objective coherence [is really and truly] gone."

Gestalt Psychology

As a case in point, consider the fate of *gestalt psychology*. Founded in 1912 by two psychologists, Czechoslovak Max Wertheimer and Austrian Wolfgang Köhler, this theory of perception contended that, contrary to the verification principle, subjects can directly perceive wholly organized, coherent scenes called *gestalts*; subjects do not first sense independent and isolated sensory "patches" of, for example, primary colors they subsequently combine into (or from which they infer) complexly organized scenarios. Subjects can directly perceive "my hand holding a red ripe tomato"; they can experience a full melodic line (not just separate and distinct notes). According to gestalt psychology, in other words, the principle of verification's requirement of extreme granularity is at odds with the epistemology of sensation.

The fate of gestalt psychology with respect to philosophical epistemology and ontology was practically inevitable. Its demise is evidence of yet another missed opportunity to explore the possibility that *real intertwining* between individual entities and the environment might be capable of generating novel—and ontologically real—interdependencies—that are also perceivable as gestalts. As mentioned in the Introduction, the ripples from this blind spot are even worse: if all ontic status and causal power is bottom-up, originating solely in and with the essential properties of material point particles; if all causal relations between these are force-like and exclusively linear and deterministic, causal loops and mereological parts/whole causation being disallowed; then any resulting and apparent coherent organization must be *epiphenomenal—that is, devoid of causal power*. Any hope of ever naturalizing neuropsychology to allow emergent (semantic, cognitive, affective) properties of coordinated brain networks to play an active part in intentional causation and agency was *a fortiori* dashed. Again. As we will also see below, Elizabeth Anscombe, one of the four metaphysical heroes we will study in Part II, intuited this.

Ripples from this perspective spread broadly across academic disciplines. The fragmentation of reality that atomism brought with it went largely unnoticed because the physics-inspired presuppositions on which the theory rested went without saying. The relational ontology gestalt psychology implied was therefore never seriously entertained within mainstream Anglo-American philosophy; it struggled unsuccessfully during the mid-twentieth century against the predominance of the well-known school of psychology known as behaviorism—whose notion of stimulus-response echoed an efficient cause-effect model. Taking gestalt psychology seriously would have meant questioning the conceptual framework of epistemology—destabilizing the very scientific paradigm that practically every academic discipline was emulating. That was not going to happen. As a result, gestalt psychology's influence waned to the point of disappearance, with negative consequences for attempts to make the fact-value distinction tractable. This issue will play a prominent role in Part II, especially in the section on Anscombe's views on philosophical psychology and intentional causation. Only recently, and thanks in no small measure to the revival of a dynamical approach in experimental neuroscience, has contemporary cognitive neuropsychology begun to reanimate gestalt psychology (see Juarrero 2023 Chapter 15 for a handful of use cases).

In brief: without the "clear and distinct" Cartesian *cogito* to shackle an evil genie's power to undermine the truth of foundational sense impressions, realists fell back on a principle familiar from received Newtonian mechanics: only separate and distinct atomic elements are real and they move/change only in reaction to efficient (forceful) causes. Relations and embeddedness in context are secondary and accidental, and powerless to change anything as such. Since a binding principle among sense data points is undetectable by the sensory apparatus itself, seemingly coherent unities have only derivative status; apparent wholes—whether ontological or perceptual—are nothing but aggregates. Therefore, integrative perceptions cannot be guaranteed to mirror reality; they are constructs. Full stop.

> **THIRD FORK NOT TAKEN**
>
> Verification devolves to atomist sensory impressions—only pointillist sense data are "verifiable;" perceptual gestalts are not. Gestalt perceptual scenes are epistemic constructs, vulnerable to all manner of contextual distortions, etc. Since natural laws must be universal and eternal, perceptions cannot serve as variables of epistemic or psychological laws. See Box below.

To have proposed a viable philosophy of mind, gestalt psychology would have needed an account of how mind and world intertwine into coherent and novel wholes—in reality. It required a metaphysical account of ontological interlevel relations and that recursive "causality unknown to us" that Kant had set aside as foreign to the constitutive and determinant Reason. Absent a mereological account of causation, perceptual gestalts could not be the source of knowledge acquisition about the empirical world.

Phenomenology

Other attempts to examine the relation between perception and the world appeared as early as the late nineteenth and first decades of the twentieth century. Of these, *phenomenology* was arguably the most influential. As developed by Czech philosopher Edmund Husserl, the theory proposed to "bracket" our commonplace attitudes towards our perceptions. Bracketing was a sort of perceptual and cognitive setting-aside of some features of perceptions; the goal of bracketing was to peel away layers of presuppositions until only phenomenal experience itself remained—*as* perceived and experienced, but not "categorized." Suspending everyday judgment about whether a given object of perception faithfully represents reality as such (the noumenal realm) should allow us to better analyze the *phenomenal* (direct sensory) experience itself. Accordingly, phenomenologists maintained that stripping perceptual experience of its ordinary connotations, including its judged positive or negative valence, and focusing instead on the experience's *temperament* would sharpen our awareness of "phenomenal qualities" that suffuse and color individual perceptions, our own as well as that of others.

Phenomenology's resolutely analytic (as opposed to synthetic) approach, however, is yet another case study of positivism's unrecognized hold on Western philosophy and science's conceptual framework. Phenomenology aimed to separate the *contents* of the mind and their reference to the outside world on the one hand from the *experience's temper* or *feel* on the other—and then to devote itself to examining the latter. Phenomenology thus looked inwards solely to the experience's *felt* qualities; it assumed the temper and feel of those qualities are independent of the context in which they are experienced. This assumption allowed phenomenologists to set aside factual information about the empirical world that the perception might appear to reference.

Positivists, alas, learned the wrong lesson from this error. For them, Phenomenology's approach was too subjective. Since objective Truth was of paramount concern to the positivists, phenomenology's focus on the *attitudinal* tenor of experience led most Anglo-American philosophers to respond by gleefully consigning Husserl to departments of psychology. From our perspective today, phenomenology's approach still failed to appreciate that felt qualities are multidimensional; they are directly intertwined into contextually embedded experience.

A relational reconceptualizing of Truth conditions was never considered by either phenomenology's advocates or its critics.

Merleau-Ponty

Not so, one might retort: French philosopher Merleau-Ponty, also a phenomenologist, concentrated on the experiential qualities coming from *embodiment*, that is, of an individual's corporeal engagement with the world. Proprioceptive and interoceptive sensations are not a product of reflection or cognitive inference, he argued; they are products of a "lived" (not a physically defined and "objective") body. The thesis I have been advocating still holds, however: as expected, positivists in the Anglo-American academy dismissed Merleau-Ponty's emphasis on the *qualitative aspect of experience* conferred by embodiment—at that point positivists (as realists) were focused on the *informational content* that experience conveyed about the natural world.

At best phenomenology offered a new take on the data psychological research should study, but none of the phenomenologists proposed novel theories of the ontology of causation—that is, on how subjects become *embedded* and intertwined with each other as well as their milieu such that emergent properties arise from the integration. Desperately needed but not forthcoming was a metatheory of causation that accounted for the conditions of possibility from which there emerge *subjects*—in a lived body acting within a lived context. Without such a rethinking of ontological and epistemological foundations and presuppositions, North Atlantic philosophers at the beginning of the twentieth century treated phenomenology as just another instance of "continental philosophy."

Pragmatism

Charles Sanders Peirce

It might be surprising that *pragmatism*, the distinctly American philosophy first formulated by Charles Sanders Peirce in 1878 (*How to Make Our Ideas Clear*), did not have more of an impact among professional American philosophers. Pragmatism focused on actions directed at solving real-life problems. Rather than considering language as "a *mirror* of reality," pragmatism viewed language use as one of several *"tools"* for prediction, problem solving, and action. For Peirce, far from confirming our theories about reality by checking predictive accuracy (as we do with eclipse predictions), far from deriving universal Truths from formal deductions, the "Pragmatic Maxim" proposed to reinterpret the concept of truth in a fallibilist manner by tracking "practical consequences" of scientific hypotheses as proxies for truth-bearing (note lower-case t). By focusing, that is, on praxis, not representation or theory, it offered a metric with which to navigate the world.

To this end Peirce developed a novel, hybrid form of reasoning he called *abduction*. Reminiscent of Bayesian inference, abduction was envisioned as an iterative and recursive process of cognition and observation that complemented formal deductive inference by continuously updating the probability of an argument's premises in light of observed outcomes of an earlier prediction. From this perspective, knowledge acquisition is not a matter of sudden epiphanies, much less indelible, incorrigible sense data.

Neither is it the result of *a priori* framing. *Action in the world* is practice for continuously approximating true belief.

How was Peirce's abduction received in the halls of academia? Absent the inclusion of universal and deterministic—and analytically derived—laws of nature that underpin valid arguments with verified true premises, abduction and pragmatism went nowhere among Anglo-American professional philosophers. The analogous refrain that because no proper psycho-physical universal and deterministic laws (context be damned) have ever been formulated, mental states are not real, is still with us today.

William James

Like Peirce, American physiologist William James first conceived of pragmatism along positivist lines, as a method for clarifying concepts to dissolve metaphysical controversies. By thinking of language and cognition as *tools* for problem solving and action, James came to explicitly acknowledge that pragmatism offered a way to conceive of knowing as *interdependent with doing*. As *behavior in context, not as consequence of passive representation. Action, not just logical proof.* As an epistemological theory, pragmatism proposed intertwining the very *constitution* of knowledge with an agent's active manipulation of the world. This stance implied that reality is not ready-made out there waiting to be passively mirrored, abstractly cognized, or received in an awestruck epiphany, it is to be *experienced* and *interacted with*. In contrast to positivism's understanding of sense data as a passively received transfer of energy, *acting* in the world demands a selective interface between the outside and the inside (like eardrums—what Paul Cilliers called "active sites"). Sensory interfaces conceived in this manner negotiate the compatibility between inside and outside; on the one hand interfaces adjust input from outside. They then expel what is judged to be waste. Combined with cognitive, affective, and motor processes, sensory interfaces mutually adjust inside and outside to facilitate action in the world.

Unlike the hard sciences, pragmatists did not conclude that practical effects of particular actions underwrote universal and objective claims to absolute Truth and Falsehood. As just mentioned, pragmatists minimized the goal of reaching universal and eternal Truth—formulated in propositions, theories, and laws. *Acting in the world* warranted only tentative knowledge claims of local, provisional truths. Lower case t. Pragmatism suggested that manipulating the world captured objectively true—if local—empirical dynamics.

By conceiving of truth claims as situational and context-dependent, pragmatism arguably paved the way for the 4E approach in cognitive science (as first introduced by Varela, Thompson, and Rosch 1991 and discussed in Juarrero 2023). Even if incapable of providing the definitive "verification" (Truth guarantees) that sense datum theory allegedly promised, concrete actions whose effects and consequences asymptotically and consistently converged over time do confer some measure of justification of knowledge claims. But this opening went unrecognized for over seventy-five years. Instead, and for the same reasons as phenomenology, James's pragmatism went nowhere in American and British universities.

John Dewey, and George Herbert Mead

As formal analysis gave way to ordinary language philosophy (see below), other American pragmatists such as John Dewey and George Herbert Mead focused more directly on the impact of language on "politics, education, and other dimensions of social improvement." In these domains of collective behavior, the tools of social psychology allowed more theoretical room for context-dependent truths; when and where praxis is central, language as a "tool for problem solving and action" is more evident (*Stanford Encyclopedia of Philosophy*). So we can think of Dewey and Mead as foreshadowing Wittgenstein's ideas of *language in use* (as appeared in *Philosophical Investigations* 1953) by focusing on everyday language as used by concrete individuals in actual cultures, practices, and traditions—as used, that is, by actual agents embedded in (not just dropped into) distinct *forms of life*, especially in change-making organizations devoted to political reform, education, etc. Wherever social improvement is the mission of social organizations, it is always context-dependent. But to repeat, mainstream philosophy in the United States and Britain had no room for context-dependence because the standard model to which it subscribed had no room for two-way causal relations between parts and emergent wholes—between individual and polis. Worst of all, in economics and public policy, the physics-inspired notion of one-size-fits-all predominated.

So despite ordinary language philosophy's emphasis on "meaning in use," mainstream Anglophone academics rejected the pragmatists' emphasis on practical problem solving and concrete action in situ as resolutely as they rejected phenomenology. Consequently, pragmatism suffered pretty much the same fate as phenomenology and Freudian and gestalt psychologies: Dewey's writings were consigned to departments of education; Mead was exiled to sociology.

Remarkably, and in contrast to what was happening with positivism and its heirs in the Anglo-American academic community, continental philosophers did not ignore the coherent milieu within which human sensation and action take place. In one way or another, Freudian analysis and the many varieties of phenomenology, pragmatism, and gestalt psychology all explicitly or implicitly grappled with the significance of context — be that of the psyche, body, or social organization in question. How does context (niche, habitat, or culture) influence individual perception, knowledge acquisition, and knowledge structure? How can an individual's perception and action in turn influence that context? Unlike their Anglo-American counterparts, European philosophers and the schools they founded did acknowledge the significance of the relation between persons and the *embedding* environment in which they are situated. Once again, not plunked into, but embedded in. Today we would call that relation a form of *framing* — how an overarching environment — be it linguistic tradition, family dynamics, or cultural practices and rituals — self-organizes such that the sensory, cognitive, and affective states of those individuals born and conditioned into that context are shaped into processes that are interdependent with that milieu. How do interdependent totalities enabled by such constraints form such that the individual components are in turn constrained by the wholes? Is this way of thinking the outcome when wars are fought on one's territory? I think of this problem whenever I point out to Vietnamese friends, "Well, Vietnam still restricts freedom of expression and freedom of speech. Isn't that terrible?" The unvarying answer is, "Anything is better than war."

To sum up: evidence ranging from the biosphere to human psychology increasingly shows that parts and wholes mutually adapt and co-evolve. Husserl tried to set aside that framing by focusing on the qualities of interiority, of the "phenomenological" aspects of experience; Merleau-Ponty quickly brought context back into the picture by emphasizing bodily experience. But with the positivist paradigm firmly entrenched, such context-dependent ideas were nonstarters because, once again, a metatheory of mereological causation was not on offer.

Chapter 3

Track 2
What is Goodness and How Do We Know it?

The exclusive emphasis on logical proof and empirical verification that permeated logical positivism naturally led to concerns about the relationship between fact and value (moral or otherwise). This was especially true given the near universal adoption in Anglo-American philosophical circles of Hume's conclusion that "you cannot [logically] derive an *ought* from an *is*." This thesis sundered reality into two irreducible realms—not mind and matter *à la* Descartes, but fact and value. How to understand the relationship between value and empirical reality within a positivist framework? What is value—specifically, *moral* value—and how can we know it?

Half a century earlier, Cambridge Apostle G.E. Moore (1903) had proposed a theory known as *ethical non-naturalism*. This was a purportedly realist (but non-natural) theory that proposed that the terms "goodness" and "rightness" refer to objective qualities in the world. The adjective *Good*, Moore argued, picks out a property that is objectively real. But it is *non-natural* because value cannot be *defined* in terms of observable features. Analytic sentences like "*This triangle has three sides"* are tautologies: their predicates repeat the content of the subject. As such their syntax tells you nothing new about the world; they are necessarily true but lack empirical content. Defining goodness in terms of an empirically observable property such as pleasure-producing, as utilitarianism proposed, Moore argued, would turn the claim, "Anything that is good is utility/pleasure producing" into an analytic truth. Like the proposition "Triangles have three sides," it would be necessarily true but uninformative about the world.

But alleged definitions of moral worth are not uninformative. They leave room for meaningful but open questions about the relation between morality and the world—questions, Moore argued, like "Ah, but is it *good* that moral value is utility-producing/pleasant?"

From these considerations Moore concluded that attributions of moral value are not analytic; they convey information about the world that goes beyond any possible definition. Judgments of moral worth assign real qualities to actions and events. Such *moral qualities* are not accidental; they identify and individuate actions and events as valuable, as *worthy* of our approval. Crucially, Moore insisted that although the action in question might be empirically observable and measurable, *its value as such* is not *observable, detectable,* or otherwise quantifiable through the senses or empirical experimentation. His conclusion: moral qualities are real but *non-natural*.

Moral Intuitionism

So, if not by sensory or experimental detection, by what epistemic process do humans apprehend these non-natural moral *qualities*? How did realist philosophers from the eighteenth century until the First World War think that the qualities of goodness and rightness are gleaned? How do human beings grasp moral *worth*?

Over a century earlier, Hume's fellow Edinburgher Adam Smith's *The Theory of Moral Sentiments* (1759) had addressed Hume's dichotomy between facts and values by attributing the human capacity to apprehend moral value to *our nature as social beings*. Smith understood human sentiments to be a product of *social psychology*. In other words, he implicitly understood that our cognition of value is intimately tied to our interconnectedness. Readers can see where this is going: by the early decades of the twentieth century this claim was a nonstarter because in a Newton-inspired and mechanics-informed worldview the very idea of "social being" does not pick out a real property. From a mechanistic perspective, it is contradictory to suggest that *internal essences* are at their very core *interdependent with facts in the environment*, much less with the social fabric. In Newtonian science there is no causal mechanism capable of generating real—i.e., causally powerful—collective dynamics we know as social organizations and cultures. Much less interweaving these into individual cognitive capabilities that represent embeddedness in context. (In the twentieth century, complexity theorists felt vindicated by the discovery of epigenetics precisely over this very issue.)

In keeping with a longstanding British tradition of *intuitionism*, Oxford philosophers and self-proclaimed realists H.A. Prichard (1912) and the much younger and W.D. Ross (1930) boldly accepted G.E. Moore's realist mantle. They proposed that human beings can cognize objective value directly. For Moore, Prichard, and Ross, moral qualities are real, non-natural, and inherent in events and actions themselves—but critically, they can also be apprehended by a distinctly human faculty, *moral intuition*.

This non-sensory but epistemic capability can identify (non-natural) qualities in the world. (I am tempted to say, for *non-natural* read *non-material* or *stuff-like*, which went together with the uncritically accepted assumption that fundamentally all reality is physical and thing-like.) So how to provide a naturally realist account of such moral intuition, especially since by the early twentieth century there was no unseeing the advances of modern physics or Frege's warning about relying on intuition?

In an interesting attempt to conform to causality as energetic transfer, Prichard and Moore proposed that moral intuition was analogous to *ordinary vision*: somewhat like the ability of dogs to hear sounds beyond the range of human hearing, moral value in the world (which, as realists, they held to be independent of the cognizer) could impress itself on the human mind. The source of the sound or the morality is out there independent of the dog or its human owner, respectively, but their essential natures allow them to selectively perceive it.

The analogy is particularly brittle precisely because of the role that *attunement* to context plays in our grasp of moral value. Canines have an innate ability to hear high decibel sounds *without training or attunement*. In contrast, as M&W correctly note, the notion of moral *intuition* implies that for this postulated faculty to work effectively, the subject must be "especially *attuned to* reality's moral features" (p. 42). Without having to mention the problems we encountered in the previous chapter occasioned by an ultra-granular understanding of sense data, developing the capacity for *intuiting* moral worth is therefore unlike the capacity for sight or hearing: specifically, observing patterns of light or sound waves does not require prior training, conditioning, or habituation. In contrast to bare sensory perception (and as we shall see in the section on prescriptivism below), acquiring *moral sensitivity* does. It requires being enmeshed in (not just plunked into) a distinctive social milieu. It is more like an apprenticeship program that develops a complex skill; it implies that the individual has become intertwined with certain features of that milieu. It is a form of en-training, as with sheep dogs who appear to go beyond mere stimulus–response conditioning and *understand* the *meaning* of dozens of commands. Immersion and embeddedness in a milieu, niche, habitat, or ecosystem—or a culture—are not automatic. Attunement to context is the achieved outcome of both a process of phylogenetic evolution and of individual learning, training, and especially acculturation.

In other words, sensitivity and attunement at the species and individual levels are contingent upon developing interdependencies with a community's (or niche's, or habitat's) multi-layered practices, traditions, rituals, expectations, and so on. Discerning which features are *relevant* (morally or axiologically in general, to this moment and set of circumstances, and which not) is not automatic. Understanding relevance goes beyond stimulus–response habituation. It is a sort of fitting together with the context to grasp emergent features of the enhanced systemic whole. Just as natural selection fine-tunes that intertwining with the environment (think the attunement of bird migration patterns to the amount of sunlight or heat), a human being's sensitivity and capacity to grasp distinctly moral features in the world is fine-tuned not only by natural selection; it is also *refined* and specified through acculturation and education, by *learning* which properties of which situations are *relevant to evaluative considerations* and which are not. In the individual, developing such sensitivity presumably requires a more or less lengthy process of uniquely moral sensitization akin to apprenticeship—iterated trial and error interactions that over time shape a discerning attentiveness and responsiveness to a combination of empirical and distinctly context-dependent and task-relevant (in this case *moral)* conditions that are co-present in the situation. As we will see below, Philippa Foot (1959) and Martha Nussbaum (2011) argued that the important value-laden relations between individuals and the spatiotemporal context in which they are embedded are those directly pertinent to human flourishing.

Phylogenetically, such attunement to context requires a lengthy process of selection—that is why natural selection amounts to the fitting together of individual and temporally extended lineage or tradition. Acquiring the sense of moral intuition is therefore analogous to developing a theory of mind (ToM), the social skills children 3–4 years old develop as they come to grasp cognitively that others may have beliefs and feelings different from their own and to adjust their expectations accordingly. It is a skill that does not appear in abused children isolated from contact with others. Despite its non-observable "nature," such intertwining is nevertheless shaped in response to the actions and reactions of others—in a particular set of circumstances, and from a specific and intentional frame of mind.

Moral sensitivity, we might say, develops as a result of extended periods of "fitting together" of individual to social organization, be it family, religion or culture, city, or state. Social norms in turn are features of collective dynamics as manifest in its members, consequent to a parallel process of the co-adaptation and co-evolution of species to niche and habitat via natural selection. All this suggests that the non-natural but objectively real moral qualities Moore was groping for are *systemic* properties, relational, broadly understood, and formed by intertwining constrained individuals, events, and processes into an overarching social web or network into which the individuals become entrained. And from which emerge axiological properties not accessible via sensory faculties to detect matter and energy. How does this process occur in human society, in human perception? What are the enabling conditions, the affordances, that generate such social learning and sensitivity? And most importantly, what is the "causal" mechanism that embeds individual into an *umwelt*—a niche or habitat, or a culture—such that learning and moral sensitivity are even possible?

Efficient causality alone cannot account for this process. Unfortunately, Moore had no theory of mereological relations to offer in its stead.

By the late 1920s, Moore's hypothesis about non-natural qualities and their apprehension just came across as unscientific mumbo jumbo. Prichard's intuitionism too seemed to harken back to old-fashioned idealist illumination. The whole approach gave off a whiff of circular reasoning: appealing to a mysterious and non-empirically ascertainable faculty of moral intuition just snuck in socially informed sentiments and sympathies through the back door. And in any case, to repeat, any appeal to moral intuition accounted only for the epistemic side of the equation: there was, to repeat, no accompanying metaphysics of causation to explain the process of *acculturation*, the social and psychological process of fitting together individual and systemic whole. Newtonian science could not explain whereby interlocking interdependencies among individual entities generate collective dynamics with emergent properties including axiological—and even moral—ones. Even less did the received physics of the day explain how these interdependencies exert influence both bottom-up and top-down—*from* constrained interactions among individuals *on* culture and *from* social dynamics *on* individual members. As we saw in the previous chapter, according to positivism perception of any sort had to be explained in terms of efficient causality among independent particles in response to forceful collisions.

The lingering horrific effects of World War I and the ongoing worldwide economic Depression slowly undermined logical positivism's theoretical vacuum with respect to value, especially moral value. Nevertheless, it would be years before the topic of mereology would explicitly surface in professional philosophy circles. Instead of taking socio-economic context seriously, academic philosophy in the United States and Great Britain sidestepped the issue altogether by offering up two metaethical theories, *emotivism* and *prescriptivism*. The next two sections briefly outline how that story went bad.

Emotivism

It is often said that Ayer's logical positivism and the verifiability principle viewed human beings as "calculating machines" but, as just mentioned, suspicion was growing that no formal analysis or deductive logical proofs could account for the full richness of reality. In view of the gradual demise of Moore's non-naturalism decades earlier, the ball was in positivism's court to offer its own positive account of moral value.

A.J. Ayer complied.

Alongside its dismissal of metaphysical, religious, and theological statements as described above in Chapter 2, Ayer's 1936 positivist booklet *Language, Truth and Logic* proposed a companion metaethical theory about value judgments. It promised to do for metaethics what formal logical analysis had done for metaphysics.

In that manifesto (remarkably published in the midst of the most severe global depression the world has ever experienced), Ayer maintained that statements such as "Murder is wrong" might *appear*, as Moore had argued decades earlier, to attribute objectively real, if unobservable, moral qualities to human actions. But as with metaphysical or religious pronouncements, logically analyzing the concepts of *value, good, right,* or *wrong* as used in everyday language reveals their true import to be otherwise: to paraphrase Ayer (who was in turn paraphrasing Hume) — when I act (or see, hear about) others acting in a certain way (being kind to others, truthful, etc.) those experiences are *accompanied* by positive feelings; other type of actions are likewise accompanied by different, negative, feelings. But human perception cannot empirically *sense* moral qualities in the actions or events themselves. Faced with this empiricist paradox, and unlike either Moore's earlier pivot to non-natural properties and intuition or Adam Smith's reintroduction of natural human empathy elicited by social psychology, Ayer contradicted the major premise common to intuitionism and Adam Smith. Ayer's conclusion: *if there are no observable characteristics common to all cases, moral properties cannot be intuited nor directly sensed,* he reasoned.

Consequently, moral attributions should be withdrawn altogether from the domain of empirical statements and reclassified as expressions of taste and preference.

And with that one quick hand flap Ayer dismissed moral value from the world. One would think that the evident suffering of people at soup kitchens throughout the Western world would have elicited a different reaction. It didn't. Far from relating moral value to social conditions, Anglo-American philosophers from the 1930s through mid-century avoided a direct confrontation with the fact–value distinction.

Interestingly, however, Ayer conceded that:

- Although unlike metaphysical or theological statements, which formal analysis revealed to be completely meaningless, utterances expressing *moral judgments are indeed meaningful*.
- However, they are meaningful only as expressions of feelings and encouragement of motivation. Therefore,
- *Since the verifiability principle covers only declarative statements, it does not apply to moral statements.*

Crudely put: according to Ayer, everyday commonsense phrases such as *X is good* or *Doing Y is right* are meaningful —they are not nonsensical gibberish as metaphysical statements are. But neither are they declarative sentences; they do not state propositions about matters of fact within the purview of rational deliberation. Nor do they state falsehoods. *Ethical statements are neither correct or incorrect, true or false, because they are not declarative and therefore do not even state facts. They belong not to the domain of knowledge but to the domain of the sentiments.* But not social sentiments à la Adam Smith.

Instead, A.J. Ayer declared that moral pronouncements are like the grunts of weightlifters at the gym, their purpose being either to encourage the speakers themselves and/or dissuade listeners to perform or refrain from certain actions. In brief, statements of moral judgments are tantamount to emotive outbursts, mere *expressions* of attitudes and emotions. As such they are exempt from the requirement of verification. Decades later these kinds of concepts would be labeled *performatives*.

Ayer's positivist metaethical theory came to be known as *emotivism*.

3. Track 2

> **FOURTH AND FIFTH ROADS NOT TAKEN**
>
> 1. Moore's Goodness as a non-natural moral quality was ascribed to the event or character itself instead of as feature that emerges in the interactions between individual and group.
>
> 2. Prichard and Ross reconceptualized *moral intuitionism* like "ordinary vision but a form of vision especially attuned to moral features" and modulated by "sensitivity to social context." But with no supporting account of a causal mechanism that creates such an interface between individual and social context—and faced with the conflicts in moral intuition over the same type of action—the theory faded after the Second World War.

Emotivism dissolved the fact–value problem by falsifying the first horn of the dilemma: because moral pronouncements are not declarative, they state nothing about the real world. Therefore, they can be neither true nor false. They have no need for verification any more than a grunt does; consequently they are exempt from the requirement of empirical validation. The verification principle does not apply to statements about (purported) moral value.

To put emotivism into historical context: as befitted the received atomist and reductionist framework of the era's physics, following natural scientists such as Heisenberg, Bohr, and Born in holding fast to positivism (see Artigiani 2021 on Labatut), ordinary language analysis proposed that moral language does not pick out real (read sensorily detectable) properties at all (natural or otherwise). Such utterances merely vent the speaker's preferences and try to get the listener to feel the same. Allegedly moral "judgments" are more like emotional eruptions no different from encouraging cheers and discouraging jeers at sporting events.

Critically, this implies that rational deliberation is no part of ethical judgment at all. There is no reasoning about ethical values.

Ayer's emotivism was almost inevitable. Logically deducing an evaluative conclusion by reasoning from empirical premises was no longer possible after Hume closed off the option of deriving moral evaluations from factual premises. Add to that Frege's general dismissal of intuition generally, which perforce eliminated moral intuition. Combined with the insistence on sense datum level granularity, perception uncovers no detectable qualities in behavior or events. Conclusion: moral *judgments* are not judgments at all; they are expressions of preference that by masquerading as an objective judgment (Lipscomb 2021, p. 93) can be uttered as "a form of manipulation" to "pressure listeners to conform to the speaker's attitude" — somewhat like parents saying to their three-year-old, "We do want to share, don't we?" To make matters worse, emotivism was non-falsifiable: given that there is no disputing about taste, no rational objections are possible. Hence there is no reasoning about value claims.

Emotivism quickly came to be caricatured as the theory that held that moral statements are equivalent to "X, Hoorah!" or "Y, Boo!" Its appeal began to fade after the horrors of the Second World War were publicized and Stalin's atrocities were made public.

Ordinary Language Philosophy

After World War II, *ordinary language* philosophy (more generally known as analytic philosophy *tout court*) became the reigning school of philosophy in Anglo-American departments of philosophy. This new approach turned away from formal logic and looked instead for guidance from *Philosophical Investigations* (*PI* 1953), Wittgenstein's second book in which he favored a more commonplace understanding of language—language as it is used in everyday life. A possibly apocryphal anecdote about how this conversion came about is telling: Ray Monk, it is said, asked Wittgenstein how the Italian chin flick gesture transmitted *a logical picture of facts*. In response, so the story goes, Wittgenstein turned his back on the logical picture theory of language of the *Tractatus* and proposed that meanings of utterances are elucidated not through formal syntactical analysis that uncovers the logical picture expressed in its syntax. Unlike the *Tractatus*, the *PI* did not attempt to tease semantics out of syntax; it implicated semantics directly—the meaning of a sentence is revealed in the way it is used in everyday conversation. Philosophers should ask, "What do we mean by ... in ordinary language?" Analyzing *meaning as use* meant examining ordinary statements uttered by real persons embedded in a particular *form of life*.

Replacing formal logic, ordinary language and those forms of life in which linguistic practices take place enlarged realism's theater of operations. J.L. Austin, Britain's most famous ordinary language philosopher, was known for responding to practically any controversial philosophical debate with the question, "And what do you mean by that?" "What do we mean by [*that statement*]?" became the rallying cry of Anglo-American analytic philosophy by the early 1950s.

That this approach takes for granted the context in which language is used was often not even recognized: the fact that everyday language use in concrete forms of life carries with it at all times weighty contextual (read cultural) baggage was not directly addressed. Pointedly, that is, the exact scope of reference of the *we* in "What do we mean by ..." was taken for granted at the time. British and American philosophers of the period took for granted that *we* referred to *people like us* — with the added supposition that only *we* are transparent mirrors of reality. That the pronoun itself might be an indefinite pronoun and not a personal pronoun that refers to members of a clearly defined group was never questioned; that *we* might as easily refer to women or individuals of other races — more generally, to individuals *in other cultures, with different personal and cultural — different epigenetic! — histories*, whose practices and mindset are informed by a different and specific socioeconomic history — this did not occur to the homogeneous group of hyper-educated, Northern European males that at the time comprised the faculty of British and American university philosophy departments. Both of these objections clearly foreground the role of social context in moral judgments (in ordinary parlance and even in emotive preferences) — but once again, that possibility was simply not raised in the Anglo-American philosophy departments for decades. In contrast, say, to the issues the Moroccan independence movement at least raised for French consciousness, the cultural insensitivity in evidence by the British of partition of the subcontinent is stark. The 1960s Civil Rights movement and the Vietnam War changed all that.

"Whose ordinary language?" From this blind spot of Anglo-American ordinary language philosophy one can almost predict today's culture wars. As someone who is fully bilingual and bicultural, I often witness two individuals using dictionary-proper language but totally failing to communicate. The words might be familiar, but neither is "getting" what the other is trying to say.

The Anglo-American transformation from formal analysis and logical positivism to ordinary language (analytic) philosophy did not overturn Hume's fact–value distinction. The possibility that a Japanese officer could just as easily dismiss torture of Western POWs by asking *his* fellow compatriots, "And what do *we* mean by asserting that our treatment of POWs is morally right?" and receive nearly identical answers from *his* countrypeople opened a slippery slope towards moral relativism. (We will examine the role of thick concepts like "torture" in Part II.) But once again, in yet another refusal to take advantage of an opening to a context-dependent understanding of reality, British and American philosophers simply turned away from exploring intertwined relations between specific environmental and historical contexts and the linguistic practices of concrete language users embedded in those contexts. Context matters because of its consequences: the insensitivity to all manner of context with which the partition of British India in 1947 was carried out reflected ignorance and disparagement of local conditions. It would be followed in subsequent decades by independence movements worldwide, usually with similarly horrific atrocities.

By the end of the Second World War, the egregious blind spots of emotivism were unacceptable. The controversy over facts and values had been challenging the mindset at Oxford and Cambridge. In contrast to the United States, which did not see combat on its own soil, during the First World War students at Oxford and Cambridge had repeatedly encountered patients suffering from trench warfare-induced post-traumatic stress disorder who were living in campus buildings-turned hospitals. In the years between 1936 when Ayer's *Language, Truth and Logic* appeared and the close of the Second World War, the bombings of civilians in Guernica, Spain, compounded by stories of the 1938 Kristallnacht violence narrated by fellow students exiled from the Nazi regime, contributed to turning the tide against emotivism. After the war, the impact of photographs of emaciated prisoners liberated from Nazi camps and of civilians suffering from radiation burns from the bombings at Hiroshima and Nagasaki was decisive. The shock produced by the devastating newsreels of dazed Nazi camp survivors and Japanese-held Allied POWs shown in neighborhood movie theaters was as horrific back then as television footage of the Vietnam war invading American living rooms would be decades later — or the torture at Abu Ghraib 30 years after that.

The distinctly moral condemnation these images provoked could not easily be dismissed as emotional venting — "Torture, Boo!" Before the Second World War the modern-sounding notion that metaphysics is a hold-over from earlier unenlightened times was acceptable to a science-enamored audience. At the time (especially in response to the visual tricks of Impressionism and the shock of abstract art generally), even the claim that aesthetic judgments are subjective felt modern. But... *De gustibus non est disputandum* was well and fine for matters of taste, even art. But morality? Moral judgments strongly imply that rational considerations are at the center of any attribution of rightness or wrongness, good and evil; in contrast, reflection and deliberation are not present in evaluations of food preferences. After the horrors of World War II, putting "torture is wrong" in the same epistemic category as "this pudding tastes awful" just went too far.

After World War II academic philosophy was afforded yet another opportunity to confront the fact–value dichotomy head-on by acknowledging the role context plays in attributions of value. How did it respond? Another missed opportunity: Anglo-American philosophy replaced Ayer's emotivism with R.M. Hare's *prescriptivism*.

It would be wrong to infer from the above that male philosophers at Oxford and Cambridge remained on the sidelines during the Second World War. Most served, in a variety of capacities: Peter Strawson served with the Royal Electrical and Mechanical Engineers; Anscombe's husband, Peter Geach, a conscientious objector, was employed in timber production. Wittgenstein worked as a porter at a hospital in London during the Blitz. Two were centrally involved in intelligence work: A.J. Ayer distinguished himself as an intelligence officer in the Welsh Guards, primarily as a Special Operations Executive and with MI6. J.L. Austin, a member of the British Intelligence Corps, directed nearly 500 analysts with the logistics for D-Day. The thoroughness of Austin's knowledge of the coastal defenses in northern France and the detailed reports supplied by his section are often cited as one of the primary factors for D-Day's success.

As far as I can tell, however, the only academic philosopher who brought to bear his wartime experiences in his professional publications was Oxford tutor R.M. Hare. During the grueling march up the River Kwai as part of a crew of POW officers tasked with building the railway from Siam to Burma (Thailand to Myanmar), Hare began jotting down notes in a journal. Once the railway was completed, he remained imprisoned with other Allied officers in Singapore until the war ended. In his journal Hare described the cruelty and horrific conditions the prisoners experienced under Japanese occupation; remarkably, however, in his autobiography Hare explicitly stated that he preferred "to pass over our sufferings during the eight months we were there." Nevertheless, testimony from others and even informal comments by Hare himself describe the Allied prisoners' *incomprehension*—their surprise—of the Japanese officers' positive attitudes towards camp conditions.

Near starvation rations, physical and mental torture, and arbitrary executions that routinely took place in those camps elicited questions about the reality of objective moral value and how human beings come to apprehend it. Steeped in the legacy of positivism, R.M. Hare was one of those prisoners. As we saw above, however, emotivism had closed off the very possibility of objective moral truth by denying that rational deliberation played any role in apprehending moral value. Are judgments reducible to emotional outbursts? If one individual reacts with "Hurrah!" to the same actions and events to which another reacts with "Boo!," are there no objective considerations in virtue of which those acts can be rationally judged morally right or wrong? Can no *reasons* be given that support one or the other evaluation?

Images of concentration camps and nuclear bombings moved students and tutors to do something about emotivism; it was imperative to give some account of the cognitive, rational aspect of moral judgments.

Prescriptivism

Hare's response, published as *Language of Morals* (1952), was a metaethical theory called *universal prescriptivism*.

As remarkable as it may seem today, prescriptivism doubled down on the bedrock foundation of emotivism, albeit with an added Kantian twist. It continued to subscribe to emotivism's staunch adherence to positivism's thesis that moral statements like "Murder is wrong" are exempt from empirical verification; prescriptivism concurred that attributions of moral value are not declarative statements about objective value-informing properties ("rightness" or "wrongness") in empirically observable events or processes. But prescriptivism deviated from emotivism in holding that neither do moral statements reduce solely to emotive regurgitations or encouraging outbursts like a wrestler's grunts. As a former prisoner of war Hare was well aware that emotivism launched ethics on the slippery slope to moral relativism, a philosophical position he clearly wanted to avoid.

Hare's original insight was that the metaethical pronouncements of emotivism *contradicted* ordinary language usage. Instead of consisting of emotional outbursts, and even if they do not constitute statements of fact, ordinary language statements purporting to express moral *judgments* serve not merely as encouragement or dissuasion to certain behaviors. They proffer *imperatives or guidelines that direct, advise, and/or command* listeners (including the speakers themselves) *to perform or refrain from* certain kinds of action. That is, Hare agreed with Ayer that moral statements do not belong to the declarative realm; they remain *performatives*. His difference with emotivism, however, is critical: expressions of preferences are unproblematically variable: since they are not declarative statements there is no *reasoning in matters of taste*; I do not contradict myself if I detested the taste of artichokes years ago but I love artichokes now. In contrast, however, Hare maintained that *moral judgments as used in ordinary language are implicitly universal*. They carry authority insofar as they commit the speaker to being consistent.

What does prescriptivism's universalizability requirement for moral judgment and behavior amount to? At a minimum, Hare implied, common usage of moral terms disallows both full-blown situationism and exceptions in one's favor. Speakers who utter moral pronouncements, in other words, implicitly commit to prescribing the same imperative for any relevantly similar act performed in relevantly similar circumstances, *including by the speaker*. As a survivor of a POW camp Hare was evidently searching for evaluative judgments that transcend local circumstances and custom; he was searching for attributions of value that go beyond local usage (*façons de parler*) — and practices — and as such can underpin non-arbitrary and universal moral commandments. As a product of the Oxfordian world of ordinary language philosophy, Hare noted that norms of ordinary language usage commit anyone pronouncing utterances like "Murder is wrong" to be *consistent*. To that extent Hare was just echoing Kant's renowned categorical imperative: users of ordinary language who state "Keeping promises is right" commit to consistency regardless of whether the promise is theirs or someone else's. Those who state "This kind of treatment of prisoners of war is right" commits to being treated that way themselves. Unlike the language of taste, that is, the *language of morals* has an internally self-consistent logic of its own. If all conditions are relevantly similar, moral judgments must be consistent to qualify as moral. This is what is meant by a "principled" life, a call to live in engaged and consistent *commitment* to a particular way of life. Hare's universalizability thus responded to the age-old philosophical concern of "How should I live my life?" by arguing that (at the very least) moral worth is emphatically absent in weathervane swings of changing opinions and dispositions. The devil is in the detail: "What counts as *relevantly similar*?" A question never addressed at that time.

Is the universalizability in Kant's categorical imperative different from the consistency requirement of Hare's prescriptivism? Kant, in the end analysis, was an idealist who believed that the so-called "Moral Law within" is an eternal and universal feature of reality which we apprehend in a sort of epiphanic illumination. In contrast, Hare concurred with emotivism that there exists no empirically identifiable feature in the world that makes any given behavior *objectively* right or wrong, much less universally and eternally so.

At best, then, the implied universality of Hare's prescriptivism refers to a long-lasting *personal commitment* to freely chosen principles—and therefore to a *consistent life*.

Because Oxford prescriptivism followed positivism's verificationism with respect to matters of empirical fact, Hare's universality about matters of value is only attitudinal and behavioral; it does not enact a consistency derived from either first principles or any internal logic of moral concepts or dialogical reasoning. Much less observation. It is neither metaphysical nor cognitive. Living ethically, in Hare's view, is committing to a consistent way of life. Period. Prescriptivism thus echoes existentialism's "life projects": "You create meaning by choosing a set of principles and living by them." It is an executive function. As Lipscomb notes, however, in neither prescriptivism nor existentialism *is there any "deeper reality" underpinning the "principles" or "commitment"* (Lipscomb 2021, p. 96). The decision is not based on reasons; consistency itself, in other words, is the only principle. And only as a sense-making framework. For oneself.

To repeat, prescriptivism provides no rational justification for adopting one principle over any other. Years ago, a banker I very much loved and respected would always preach to me that "government bailouts are wrong." When President Ford famously refused to come to the assistance of NY City (whose bonds the banker had advised his superiors to purchase), I immediately phoned him. "Well, what do you think of government bailouts now?" To his credit he replied, "If it was wrong then it would be wrong now, even if I and my bank stand to lose a lot of money." I admired that banker's consistent, principled stance, but, like Moore, I could still ask, "Oh, but was he right?" Was my father right?

As we will see in Part II, Iris Murdoch's early admiration for existentialist novels would not be shared by her fellow philosophers back at Oxford. And she knew it. In contrast, Hare's attempt to repackage existentialist principles to a "committed life" into Anglo-American ordinary language philosophy fared somewhat better, but not for long. Why? In retrospect we can appreciate that both prescriptivism and existentialism suffer from the same critical flaw: as long as agents are consistent, neither theory offers objective considerations that could provide a rational basis of choosing one as morally different from another: from a prescriptivist perspective, what is to prevent perfectly consistent sadomasochists from committing to a life devoted to inflicting pain?

Once again readers can read between the lines: in light of the Academy's refusal to accept that context can have causal consequences, Hare's conclusion was inevitable. When relevant biological and social constraints are set aside (whether because of the received atomistic ontology or modernity's understanding of causality as exclusively energetic transfer), then context plays no role in grounding moral reasoning by providing evidence in favor or against one alternative over another. Sometimes sociocultural context can be ignored with no repercussions—like Galileo dismissing friction when studying gravity. At other times, it takes effort or willful ignorance to set aside clearcut evidence that social constraints actively shape an individual's ideas, opinions, and beliefs; and, conversely, that the individual actions of residents, when aligned, can qualitatively change the culture's possibility landscape. Including its moral landscape.

Phrased otherwise and in keeping with Newtonian science, neither prescriptivism nor existentialism assigned proper "causal" efficacy to context—whether a biological species' niche or a human culture, much less a family's dynamic. There was no metaphysical account of how one person's actions might influence their milieu or, conversely, how that milieu might shape the individual. Both parts to whole and whole to parts relations, especially the latter as a form of top-down causation, were dismissed. Like paradigmatic existentialist heroes, therefore, Hare's moral agents are *authentic* only as atomistic free thinkers whose steady commitment to a life project is their sole constraint. Prescriptivism could not explain why Japanese POW camps' guards and American and European prisoners had different emotional reactions to the captors' actions in virtue of their upbringing (see Anscombe's views on intentional causation and agency in Part II). That the culture of each might have influenced their *individual* attitudes was not considered. Phrased otherwise: absent existentialism's starting premise that human beings find themselves thrown into a milieu—cultural, biological, or even familial—with which they have no choice but to engage, prescriptivists simply disregarded the influence that sociocultural context has on the everyday lives of their members—in particular, how established social practices and organization emerge and contribute to, prevent, or otherwise shape attitudes, prime behavior, and therefore significantly contribute to individual suffering even if those practices are of benefit to the society as a whole.

And by mid-twentieth century, there was no going back to the idea of a faculty of moral intuition that could sniff out non-natural values.

During Moore's heyday at the beginning of the twentieth century (M&W p. 43), the idea that moral value—objective *qualities* in the empirical world—could be apprehended by a natural faculty of perception was revolutionary (rather, say, than the human subject apprehending a transcendental Kantian category or moral law, or undergoing Hegelian dialectic reconciliation in a self-transcendent illumination). By the end of the Second World War, however, innate faculties of moral intuition smacked just as badly of fusty metaphysics as notions of self-transcending illuminations or non-natural intuitions. Observing how emotional reactions about the same behavior diverged dramatically worldwide made the very idea of moral intuition as suspect as Frege had cautioned.

Emotivist theory was no more palatable (pun fully intended). Concrete sociopolitical experiences swayed even diehard positivists that human beings worldwide share no emotions in common, especially with respect to moral value. Hare needed more. But in the wake of thirty-plus years of civil and world wars, as well as a global economic collapse, prescriptivism ended up faring no better; Anglo-American philosophy could offer no *reasons* for or against particular moral judgments. Not even for why consistency is valuable at all. Along with emotivism, these two metaethical theories bequeathed by positivism had nothing to say about rationally grounding moral value. They treated moral utterances as either tantamount to emotional outbursts or subjective, if consistent, commands and personal commitments.

Professional philosophy had simply abdicated its responsibility to address issues concerning lives well-lived. It had abdicated the subject matter of human flourishing.

FIFTH ROAD NOT TAKEN

After the Second World War, yet another path that would have given context its due was once again not taken. This was the clearing opened by existentialism, whose roots can be traced to German philosopher Friedrich Nietzsche and Danish philosopher Søren Kierkegaard. After the war, Frenchmen Jean-Paul Sartre and Albert Camus, Christian philosophers and theologians like Gabriel Marcel and Paul Tillich, and feminist writer Simone de Beauvoir studied the possibility of human freedom and authenticity. They all explicitly addressed the full human condition and questioned the reality of meaning and value in an absurd world. Because, for the existentialists, the human condition is summarized in the phrase *Existence precedes Essence*, meaning that individuals are first thrown into the world with no essence, they must then create meaning for themselves, by making the forging of a self-identity their *"life project."* It is through these projects that individuals understand and define themselves.

This entire approach was too incommensurate with positivism. As a result, if studied at all in the secular Anglophone academy, existentialism was usually in literature courses. That Camus and Sartre won the Nobel Prize in Literature reinforced this attitude.

Interlude

Atmosphere on Campus
from 1914–1960

From 1914 to 1960 the communities at Cambridge and Oxford universities repeatedly came face to face with sociopolitical events of a global reach unlike any even the older dons had faced before. Changing conditions at home such as women suffrage and a global depression had forced change on all sectors of society. The Russian Revolution and the Spanish Civil War raised the specter of a fascism vs. socialism faceoff. A global economic depression was unprecedented. By the end of World War II, additional moral questions raised by POW conditions in the Pacific, Nazi war camps, the nuclear bombings of Nagasaki and Hiroshima, and the Soviet occupation of Eastern Europe could not be ignored.

It wasn't just the high number of casualties among staff and students who had either volunteered or were conscripted combatants in the two wars; it was the unavoidable presence of wounded men undergoing treatment in campus buildings and sports-fields-turned-hospitals as well as those returning to campus shellshocked from trench warfare and POW detention. Significant transformations in university demographics that began after WWI only accelerated with the influx of migrants from the British colonies and the growing number of exiles from the Nazi regime. By the mid-1930s, stories of refugees from German universities who had settled in at Oxford and Cambridge (as both students and tutors) brought the real threat of a Second World War into the campus cloisters. A growing awareness that not enough had been done to support democracy and prevent the Spanish Civil War deepened this concern. Considering the more imminent threat from the Nazis, the brutal nature of the Stalinist regime was downplayed since the full extent of Stalin's atrocities (1930-1953) was not fully publicized this early—even though FDR had been made aware of the Katyn Forest Massacre of 1940.

University administrators understood that such global sociopolitical turbulence raised grave doubts about the theoretical foundations and trajectory of "Western civ," both as a curriculum and as conceptual framework. Pressure from the suffrage movement had already led Oxford to confer degrees to women in 1920 (Cambridge did so only in 1945). At Oxford, a new area of study called Philosophy, Politics and Economics (also known as Modern Greats) was an administrative innovation "born of the conviction that the study of great modern works... could transform students' intellectual lives and thereby society at large." Later, both universities created new departments of modern languages, especially in Russian and Spanish, in response to conflicts around the world.

Behind it all, in the realm of theoretical ideas, a fundamental problem with Frege's logic had been lurking for decades like *memento mori* skulls or slithery worms in still life paintings. Bertrand Russell was among the first to detect a problem with Frege's definition of abstract concepts in terms of categories and their members. In particular, Russell had noticed that in Frege's definition of numbers in terms of categories mentioned earlier, *n* is used ambiguously: it refers the first time to the *set or category itself*, the second time to the *token components* or members of the category. In 1902, almost 10 years after Frege had published *Basic Laws of Arithmetic*, Russell had written to him, "I have a problem with sets of sets." Some sets (like the set of things that are not dogs) can be members of themselves but others (like the category *humankind*) cannot—humankind is not a human. Fair enough. But what about sets like *Barbers who shave all barbers who do not shave themselves*? This was Russell's version of the ancient paradox of self-reference, the classical Cretan Liar Paradox, of which there have been many versions, including Denis Diderot's 1773 story "This is not a story" and even visual ones like Magritte's 1929 painting of a pipe titled "This is not a Pipe." How does the mind (or logic!) disentangle statements about the world from meta-statements (about statements about the world); emergent properties and causal powers of collective totalities from properties of the components or descriptions of those totalities severally? When contemplating paradoxes of self-reference, the mind does not find a resting point: it becomes trapped in an unending loop: if the sentence is true, it is false; but if it is false, it is true. Theoretically, what to do about paradoxes like these?

Dutch graphic artist M.C. Escher knew art could play with loops. Philosophy couldn't.

Russell's letter devastated Frege, who quickly realized there was no way out of philosophical problems occasioned by such paradoxes of self-reference. Frege gave up trying to correct the problem; Russell did the opposite—he devoted the following eight years to writing *Principia Mathematica*, coauthored by Alfred North Whitehead. Published in 1910, this landmark work in mathematical logic and the foundations of mathematics was the authors' heroic effort to resolve paradoxes of self-reference—to prove that mathematics can be derived from a complete and consistent system of logic; it laid the groundwork for Russell's logical atomism mentioned earlier. Along the way, *Principia Mathematica* provided the theoretical underpinning of logical positivism.

In philosophy departments across the Northern European community, the search for deductive proof steadily began to replace the search for truth. Intellectual fissures were also opening in disciplines other than philosophy. The "in principle" uncertainties sneaking into science and mathematics unsettled logicians who hoped that axiomatic systems like *Principia Mathematica*'s might ever be both consistent and complete. Published in 1931, Kurt Gödel's incompleteness theorem, especially when considered in combination with Heisenberg's uncertainty principle, proved definitively that no axiomatic system—including Boolean or Fregean formal symbolic logic itself—could, even in principle, be both consistent and complete. There would always be true meta-statements, statements *about* statements, that could not be proved within the formal axiomatic system itself. Turing took Gödel one step further by extending Gödel's ideas on incompleteness into an analysis of computability and undecidability. As Popper's falsifiability criterion would propose soon thereafter, these shocking scientific developments emerging from mathematics and formal logic had repercussions in the world of epistemology: they indirectly sounded the death knell of axiomatization and *verificationism* as the path to complete knowledge of the natural world. It took several decades for computer science, especially simulation of nonlinear processes, to provide a different door through which to understand these problems.

Meanwhile, for over thirty years, *Principia Mathematica* kept alive the hope that a fully explanatory axiomatized system was possible. Once again, the ontological possibility that constrained recursive iterations can generate emergent but very real complex dynamics, with each higher-level of coordination and description serving as context (meta-level) for goings on at the lower level… went unnoticed.

Unnoticed, that is, except by four "metaphysical" women who tried to bring philosophy back to life—to the lived experience. The something these women were *up to* and grappling with was how to incorporate the full richness of the lived experience into philosophy. The second part of this monograph summarizes the context that framed the personal and philosophical concerns of these fabulous women. And how it played out in their work.

SIXTH FORK NOT TAKEN

Taking paradoxes of self-reference lightly and assuming Russell's logico-mathematical foundations were sound promised that knowledge could result in a complete and consistent cognitive system. After Turing's groundbreaking work, algorithms that relied heavily on recursion and whose computational outcomes would reformulate the foundations of verifiability replaced the need for formal logical proof. This transition from truth and proof to the IF–THEN manipulability of algorithms naturally suggested taking a serious look at American pragmatism and Peirce's logic of abduction. But this option was for the most part ignored.

Part II

Chapter 4

The Women are Up to Something

The first two women's colleges at Oxford, Somerville and Lady Margaret Hall, were founded in 1879; two more, St. Anne and St. Hugh, had been added by the outbreak of WWII. Oxford finally admitted women as full members in 1920, thanks in part to the Victorian dons' interest in securing admission for their own daughters. It was not a complete victory: the university capped female enrollment at 20% of the undergraduate total. However, with most of the young men volunteering or recruited for the war, by late 1939 the only males on campus were older dons exempted from conscription. Finding itself short on matriculation fees and pressured by the suffrage movement, the university relaxed the 20% cap and a large number of females applied for admission. During the six wartime years between 1939 and 1945, the majority of the student body on campus were women. Ironically, the explosive growth in female enrollment rescued the finances of the men's colleges.

The sheer number of women at Oxford and Cambridge was a constant reminder that were it not for the war, a lot fewer women would be enrolled. The changes did not go unnoticed: men drinking morning coffee instead of tea was taken as evidence that "the whole atmosphere at Oxford had been 'be-womaned'" (M&W p. 19).

The in-your-face inequalities women confronted daily were unrelenting. Ater the First World War, restrictions such as going "unhatted" and some prohibitions against being "unchaperoned" had been relaxed, including the regulation requiring that male tutors meet with female students at the women's colleges rather than teaching them in the tutors' rooms. In general, however, gendered restrictions remained ubiquitous. These ranged from tables reserved for women in the dining hall—in the rear, to be sure—to the requirement that women wear skirts even under academic robes. Anscombe, who insisted on being called "Miss Anscombe" even after her marriage, famously wore only trousers. Once, after being reprimanded, she threw a skirt on over her customary trousers and exclaimed for all to hear, "I am a stickler for convention and propriety!"

Sexual harassment was common: women were routinely subject to unwanted advances. German classicist *émigré* Eduard Fraenkel as well as Freddie Ayer of emotivist fame were notorious for egregiously offensive behavior, the latter even in his mid-seventies. Midgley reports that she and Murdoch were warned that "Fraenkel will 'probably paw you about a bit, but never mind'." Subtext: Ayer says "Hoorah!" and we females say "Boo!" *De gustibus…* and all that.

Seriously?

This is all to say that the four "metaphysicals" who are the subject of this part of the book (Elizabeth Anscombe, Philippa Foot, Mary Midgley, and Iris Murdoch) could not have been unaware of the contextual shoals they had to navigate. The overall personal, social, and professional context in which the four metaphysicals lived and studied demanded unwavering attention. At minimum, as M&W

point out, they were always "on probation." And reminded of it daily: Somerville Dean Vera Farnell's welcoming remarks to incoming women routinely warned "that any misstep, any rule-breaking or scandal would injure, not only themselves but future generations of aspiring women scholars. 'You must seriously realise that women are still very much on probation in this University. You may think that it does not matter if you do something a little wild, but I can tell you that it will'" (M&W p. 17). And yet, the legacy of the four women philosophers who were indeed *on* to something offers a case study in how the absence of male students during the war years made it possible for women to "find their voice"—as philosophers in the classroom and during campus debates. In Midgley's words, "I do think that in normal times a lot of good female thinking is wasted because it simply doesn't get heard."

The four female protagonists of these noteworthy books were decidedly unconventional, and socially aware. Murdoch, who came from a "well connected Bohemian family," had joined the Communist Party of Great Britain in 1938, the same year Anscombe co-authored a pamphlet opposing Britain's entry into the forthcoming war. After reading a book on early Catholic martyrs, and despite her Anglican pastor father's threat to cut her off (he later relented), Anscombe had converted to Catholicism as a youngster. She was formally baptized at Blackfriars during her first year at Oxford. While still an undergraduate she married Peter Geach, also a Catholic and fellow philosophy student; they went on to have seven children, scandalizing many with their domestic arrangements: she often left the children in the care of Peter on one campus while she spent time on the other.

Specializing in philosophy—majoring in Greats, the degree that centered on philosophy and history—required fluency in Latin and Greek. Since most of the male students at Oxford and Cambridge were graduates of elite English "public" schools, they arrived with a strong background in those languages. By contrast, pre-college instruction of girls in Britain was not nearly as rigorous. Philippa Foot's (*née* Bosanquet) case was unusual, even for female applicants: she had received no formal education prior to matriculation in college. As a child of upper-class parents who had been married at Westminster Abbey (the daughter of US President Grover Cleveland, Philippa's mother was born in the White House), Foot was home schooled by a series of governesses from whom, in Foot's own words, she did not "learn which came first, the Romans or the Greeks." After her last governess suggested to her that she might go to college (which her parents did not expect), Foot moved to Oxford a full year before applying for admission to be tutored in classical languages. Both Mary Midgley (*née* Scrutton) and Iris Murdoch (whose preparation was also deficient in Greek and Latin) enrolled as Literature and English majors at first, and for that same reason. Like Foot and at the request of Somerville college, Midgley too devoted the year before matriculating to being coached in the two classical languages by the same former Somerville student to whom the college referred prospective students, including Murdoch (M&W p. 14).

The four became fast friends, rooming together, sharing one another's clothing—and sometimes even boyfriends.

Despite these drawbacks, Foot graduated with a degree in Philosophy, Politics and Economics (Modern Greats, the new degree mentioned earlier); Midgley's was also in Mods and Greats; Anscombe's, Foot's, and Murdoch's degrees were in Greats. Anscombe graduated with First Class Honors, Foot and Midgley with Firsts. Not bad for unprepared students.

4. The Women are Up to Something

Exempt from conscription during the war, the four women immediately joined the "war work" upon graduation in 1942 when the conflict was still raging. Foot volunteered with the Oxford Committee for Famine Relief (OXFAM) since its founding by well-known Oxford Quakers and scholars; she continued to do so after the war. In fact, Foot remained passionately devoted to OXFAM for most of her life, even serving on its Board for a number of years. She also worked in Oxford for Nuffield College's Social Reconstruction Survey, a project that aimed to link scholars with business professionals and political leaders in support of the war effort. Midgley and Murdoch joined the civil service: Midgley (more on whom later) became a secondary school teacher and did not return to campus until 1947. Murdoch, having resigned from the Communist Party in 1942, was offered and accepted a position at Treasury; she later worked in Brussels for a UN agency on refugees. (The impact of this experience on Murdoch will also be discussed below.) In contrast to the other three, Anscombe was exempted from war work even after the war because of the children. As a result, she never left academia and went to Oxford as a research student for one year after the war before returning to Cambridge to work with Wittgenstein.

When Foot, Midgley, and Murdoch returned to campus as graduate students after the war, they agreed to concentrate more directly on the role of reason in ethics. Acutely aware that one of the central legacies of positivism was to ensure that there is no "place for reason in ethics," *What do we do about Hare?* was the question to which the four women returned, repeatedly. Hare might have left raw emotivism behind and brought the need for consistency back to ethical judgment by requiring that agents commit to a form of life. But, as explained above, Hare's prescriptivism still subscribed to the thesis that evaluative judgments are not about reality. Consequently, there is no prescriptivist "disputandum" about a given choice of lifestyle because there is no "reasoning" — good, bad, or indifferent — about value.

In light of the horrors of the war and its aftermath, this conceptual impasse was unacceptable. What *do* we do about Hare?

Unlike their male counterparts in the Anglo-American philosophy establishment, who adhered to the analytic tradition for the remainder of the twentieth century, these four women, each in her own way, confronted the place of reasoning about the world and its relation to ethics head on.

Murdoch

As Lipscomb points out, Murdoch's second research proposal to the Cambridge graduate admissions committee shows that she was the first of the women to understand that philosophy needed to get beyond the fact–value distinction enshrined in positivism and its heirs, emotivism and prescriptivism. After the war, while waiting in Brussels for an assignment with the Relief and Rehabilitation Administration (UNRRA), a United Nations agency to assist displaced persons, Murdoch had grasped "how irrevocably broken so many lives have been by this war" (Lipscomb 2021, p. 108); she came to appreciate that existentialist novels by Albert Camus and Simone de Beauvoir, not yet translated into English, were "just what English philosophy needs to have injected into its veins" (*ibid.*) — a view she later repudiated after concluding that the *authentic* existentialist hero is just another version of the romantic hero. As noted, existentialism resonates with prescriptivism to the extent that both insist that individuals must take a stand and then live consistently in accordance with those freely chosen principles. Critically, however, neither theory offered reasons justifying the *content* of the commitments themselves. Existentialism and prescriptivism can be caricatured as "take a stance, any stance" views.

Even while she still subscribed to the existentialist principle that acting in good faith in the face of existential anguish was the only possible response to the horrors of World War II, Murdoch immediately grasped that "most Oxford philosophers would scorn Sartre and de Beauvoir" (*ibid.*, pp. 103–04). She was right. Despite Wittgenstein's realization that forms of life leak into utterances to make them meaningful, the very idea that philosophy might make room in its concepts for (in our terminology) context-dependence was still too *outré*. There was no room for sense-making by context. Moral pronouncements too, as we have seen, had been sidelined by emotivism and prescriptivism — by lingering ripples of positivism, as it were. They were outside the purview of rational cognition. For related reasons, as we also saw, gestalt psychology had been dismissed: the atomist foundations of contemporary physics implied that perception as such simply does not produce coherent and integrative scenarios. Similar considerations applied to Freud's notions of the subconscious and the superego. And Oxford was not about to allow novels into the canon of Western philosophy.

British philosophy's narrow understanding of what counts as philosophy proper gradually led Murdoch to drift away from professional metaphysics and metaethics to writing fiction, including poetry and plays; this modality offered more room in which to freely explore all the rich dimensions of the human condition. To explore all its sources of meaning, in other words. Murdoch left Oxford permanently in 1963 and although she continued to teach, it was not in university philosophy departments. Her deliberations about morality and politics were broadcast on regular radio talks (such as the two talks on the BBC titled "The Novelist as Metaphysician") in which she explored the relationship between existentialist fiction and philosophy.

That said, Murdoch published several rigorous analyses of philosophical concepts such as "attachment" and "displacement" in a few rare "philosophical essays." For example, in "On 'God' and 'Good'," she returns to Moore and Prichard's view that goodness is indefinable and grasped through moral intuition, a distinctly human cognitive capability to detect moral value. For the most part, however, the role that perception (or "vision") plays in moral self-transcendence is the recurring theme in Murdoch's work—fiction as well as non-fiction (Lipscomb 2021, p. 250). She explicitly discusses the importance of *paying attention*, to nature as well as oneself. Pointedly, and in contrast to her fellow analytic brethren, she thought of paying attention and perception as being open to influence by reason-giving. By either focusing narrowly or, conversely, by enlarging the scope of one's perception to a more overarching context, attention and perception can uncover the source and *raison d'être* of moral evaluations. In turn, reasons and contextual considerations thereby enlarge the subject's perceptual scope.

Murdoch often presented these philosophical dilemmas in stories with plots that turn on situations where "self-concern" stops us from treating others well. The "mother fable" is her best known: Murdoch tells the tale of how "through sustained attention" a mother can change the way she *sees* and therefore *judges* her daughter-in-law—as "not undignified but spontaneous, not noisy but gay, not tiresomely juvenile but delightfully juvenile" ("The Idea of Perfection," in *The Sovereignty of Good*, 1970, pp. 17–18).

Perception can involve reasoning and judging, which in turn can make one *see* differently. These reflections led Murdoch to conclude (as did Socrates) that "self-criticism" is a species of moral deliberation, an activity with decidedly cognitive, not solely affective, aspects. It makes it possible to "come to see more and better" — with "better" meaning "more meaningfully because more contextualized." Today we'd use the term *sense-making*.

Evaluative changes brought about by considered reflection demonstrate, in other words, that moral judgments *are* susceptible to reason — and this is not the contentless, syntactical reasoning of formal logic. Properties can change qualitatively when they are *situated* in different circumstances. Reasoning, in turn, can enlarge the context within which those considerations apply. Nowadays we call this change in perspective *reframing*: different qualities and properties are revealed, and others recede, when boundary conditions that frame a possibility landscape are enlarged or minimized. Zooming in or out will reveal or hide previously unsuspected but relevant details. However, since Anglophone academic philosophy at the time presupposed that "reason" is identical only with "formal logic" and "ordinary language analysis" — and ontology bottoms out in essential (read internal primary) particulate properties — in the eyes of Anglo-American professional philosophers Murdoch had abandoned the discipline; her work was now more suitable to literature departments.

Murdoch's prediction was therefore sadly prescient. In opposition to longstanding philosophical tradition dating back to Plato's allegory of the cave and even Einstein's penchant for *gedanken-experiments*, Oxford norms at the time would not countenance fictional narratives as serious philosophical methodology. The power of narrative sense-making to shape the way we "come to see more and better" — cognitively, not just visually — was simply not considered a rational process at the time. In consequence, Murdoch is today best known as a novelist, for works in which she infuses philosophical ideas and concerns into the plots and characters and where she explores "real moral problems" that human beings "with definite social and emotional problems face" in everyday life.

Tragically noteworthy is the fact that, despite the numerous awards those fictional writings received, including the Booker Prize (for *The Sea, the Sea*), for the rest of her life Murdoch herself felt that she did not qualify as a true "Oxford philosopher" (Lipscomb 2021, p. 110). At one point she confided to Foot that, "I am just not a philosopher" (quoted in Lipscomb 2021, p. 253). Worse: Anscombe and Foot had also concluded that Murdoch was no longer a philosopher — and for the same reason: fiction and narrative do not belong in philosophy. They would never again consider their dear friend Iris a professional member of the academy. The analytic paradigm was so deeply entrenched that even they, staunch opponents of much of the positivist agenda, followed professional norms formulated at Oxford in the early part of the twentieth century for the rest of their lives (*ibid.*, p. 251): other narrative forms of sense-making and reason-giving might qualify as literature, or moral or social psychology. But they are not philosophy. Like their male colleagues, and in what was to become a repetitive theme-and-variation motif, all four women had internalized mid-century Oxford ideas of how philosophy is done.

Foot

Anscombe and Foot's efforts to steer ethical discussions away from emotivism and prescriptivism and reintroduce context and reason in ethics were indeed "better framed for the guild" (Lipscomb 2021) than Murdoch's forays into fiction and fables. Better framed even than Midgley's later mucking about in biology, as I will describe below.

Foot's articles were the first to confront prescriptivism head-on in professional publications (*ibid.*). She and Anscombe often discussed the theoretical potential of *"thick concepts,"* which Anscombe had first heard about from Wittgenstein (*ibid.*, p. 101). In retrospect, their conversations on this topic were evidently conducted against the background of prescriptivism's manner of dealing with the fact-value problem, not to mention the backdrop of Oxfordian professional norms. Anscombe and Foot agreed, terms like "good" and "right" are *thin* when used in a moral context by ordinary people; they do not clearly identify which concrete actions are right and which are not because the criteria for their use are too vague and imprecise. It is unclear when their usage is warranted in daily life. In contrast, concepts like "friendship," "rudeness," "cruelty," "courage," and "compassion" are *thick in the sense that in addition to their evaluative aspect they build-in reference to a descriptive component.*

Thick concepts and their implications for ethics would interest Foot for the rest of her life. In what became her signature theme, she often returned to analyze "what we mean" by "thick [moral] concepts" in general. She came to the realization that *in each case the evaluative aspect of the character or action is interdependent with and contingent upon empirically ascertainable facts of the matter.* More to the point, usage of thick terms in everyday language shows that those concepts are not identical with expressions of brute emotions and arbitrary preference, no matter how consistently deployed. Moral language is different from both emotivist venting and prescriptivist commanding.

Foot's insight was that thick concepts weave particular empirical conditions into value judgments. By implying the co-presence of specific empirical facts, the meaning and ordinary usage of *thick concepts intertwine descriptive and valuational aspects.* The revolutionary implication of this approach is that folding matters of fact into the ordinary language usage of evaluative terms like "right" and "good" blurs the fact–value distinction and thereby undercuts the argument in favor of emotivism and prescriptivism. It also undermines the claim that ordinary language's usage of moral terms does not implicate facts. Foot had found a way to adhere to the methodology of ordinary language philosophy while making room for verification of empirical statements. How? By showing that *it is in virtue of the empirical verifiability of the descriptive component of thick concepts that they carry evaluative heft in ordinary language.*

Thick concepts, that is, blur the fact–value distinction by putting the lie to emotivism's and prescriptivism's sharp dichotomy between description and evaluation. They also and felicitously falsify Hume's principle that one cannot derive an "ought" from an "is." To the contrary, ethical judgments are *justified by the empirical facts and conditions* the moral terms imply.

The next step in this novel approach to metaethics was to note that the facts-of-the-matter implied by thick moral concepts necessarily refer to conditions that contribute to or detract from *human flourishing*. To illustrate this point, Foot was among the first to point out that threats to human flourishing underpin classical virtues like *temperance* and *prudence*. When used in a moral context, the proper usage (and definition) of thick terms implicitly refers to the action's potential to enhance (or diminish) human well-being—*which potential is ascertainable as an empirical matter of fact*. For example, calling someone *courageous* implies the presence of a certain attitude, or the performance of certain actions *in the face of significant danger*. It is grammatically screwy to call someone *courageous* — actions *cannot be* courageous — if there is no factual threat to life or bodily harm. It is likewise linguistically incorrect to call someone *cruel* whose behavior causes no hurt; attributions of *cruelty* (or compassion, kindness, and so on) logically presuppose a negative (positive) impact on the recipient's well-being. The behavior of a temperate or prudent person cannot be a statistical outlier. And so on. Foot was also the first to understand the significance of how, in an iterative spiral, *the evaluative aspect of thick terms guides our behavior — and only in light of certain empirical facts, the consequences of which justify a particular evaluation.*

Other axiological (value) terms can also be thick: junk food might very well be tasty ("Junk food, Hoorah!" "Oh, no! Junk food, Boo!") and we might be remarkably consistent throughout our life in our preferences or dislikes for junk food. What is not a question of preference or matter of taste, however, is that junk food does not contribute to health — and for that reason can be objectively judged to be bad (read *unhealthy*, a normative term) for you. The concept of *nourishment*, in other words, does not refer simply to caloric intake; it is a thick concept whose embedding context would be to the item's inextricable linkage to health-promotion, a normative metric. Adequate nourishment is essential to a healthy organism, an outcome with a positive valence. Ordinary language allows calling particular foods *nourishing* only if they contribute to a healthful outcome. The positive axiological quality of the term is dependent upon the health-enhancement capabilities it builds in — in the case of nourishment, to the specific biological function to which it contributes.

In proper analytic fashion, Foot in effect turned the tables on analytic philosophy by showing that thick concepts deployed in ordinary language statements expressing value judgments have a logic—a rationale—that is absent in statements about matters of taste. In contrast to subjective preference, *distinctively ethical valuation* in ordinary language's use of moral terms deploys a logic of thick concepts and thereby implies the presence of certain empirical conditions related to human flourishing. One might even argue that prescriptivism's thesis concerning the implied universalizability of moral judgments makes sense only in light of the regular empirical correlations between certain actions and conditions that promote or detract from human flourishing. It is those regular correlations that underpin the universalizability of Kant's categorical imperative. This is not sociology; it is the folding in of facts into value. And of value into context.

I submit it is for that reason and not the reverse that value terms and utterances encourage and guide and promote certain forms of behavior: they empirically tie the behavior's relation to *worthy* outcomes.

Empirically detectable human flourishing is a necessary component of the ethical category of moral worthiness.

What would Moore have said? He could not have raised the same doubts about human flourishing that he did about defining good as pleasure: "Ah, it might contribute to human flourishing, but why is that sort of character or action right?" The factual conditions embedded in moral judgments are empirically verifiable justifications for the ascription of goodness and rightness. This was a central principle of Aristotelian ethics.

Integrating the world's facts of the matter into ethical reasoning thereby opens moral judgments to rational deliberation. In discovering the interdependence, Foot had found a role for reason and verifiability in the everyday use of thick moral concepts. Foot came to understand that Wittgenstein's "forms of life" are *umwelts* (a term Foot borrowed from Cassirer—M&W p. 281), comprehensive value-laden "worlds" in which individuals are embedded not only physically and biologically, but also, and therefore, *normatively*. Symbols and axiological principles convey empirical information about conditions for human flourishing in their normative, specifically moral, concepts and terms.

I want to emphasize that despite all-too-common misconceptions this view does not lead down a slippery slope to either relativism or subjectivism; instead, it contextualizes value judgments to empirically real conditions tied to human flourishing or degradation. In actual circumstances. One consequence of this context-dependent understanding of ethics is that "all things being equal" (*ceteris paribus*) clauses are as much needed in judgments of moral worth as in ascriptions of empirical causation (see Anscombe below) —and for the same reason: moral value is contingent on concrete empirical conditions actually contributing to or detracting from human well-being. The intersection between empirical conditions promoting or detracting from human flourishing and the appropriateness of moral judgment is precisely the domain in which reason in ethics is required. The local variability of these conditions makes concrete moral judgments inevitably context-dependent. Not subjective, context-dependent.

To summarize Foot: when existentialism and positivism "stripped metaphysics away from philosophy... the isolated subject can do nothing but choose" (M&W p. 276)— arbitrarily. This was the intolerable consequence of Hare's prescriptivism. As a professional—aka Oxfordian ordinary language—philosopher writing tracts in conformity with the guild's norms, Foot accepted that meaning is revealed by language in use. But unlike Hare, Foot noticed that thick axiological terms in everyday language carry a double load: their evaluative aspect simultaneously incorporates facts that serve as logical grounds on which the evaluation rests. Characterizing an event or action using thick terms falls within the scope of rational inference precisely because of the empirically verifiable facts involved. Indeed, this is why analyzing ordinary language suggests that human beings "rely on thick concepts to orientate ourselves in ethical relations to others" (*ibid.*). Actions fall in the purview of morality (vs. amorality) when they are performed with reference to promoting human flourishing.

But *whose* flourishing?

Why be moral if there is nothing in it for me?

According to M&W, Foot's views concerning ethical issues were a legacy she received from Oxford Professor of Moral Philosophy Donald MacKinnon, who served as wartime tutor of all four women. "His moral seriousness, his concern for the suffering of the world inspired her." Judging behavior morally—in light of its relationship to human flourishing and suffering—implies the presence or absence of certain context-dependent conditions, the "conditions of possibility" for human flourishing or suffering, so to speak. Throughout her life Foot continued to ponder whether "it still made *rational* sense to act virtuously if an agent's particular virtuous behavior would destroy their own [particular] happiness." And yet, as mentioned, and despite her lifelong concern with the world's suffering, Foot disparaged fiction as a medium for philosophical deliberation. She even spoke of admirers of "[Murdoch's 'mother fable'] … as if they must be 'feeble-minded'" (from Peter Conradi, quoted in Lipscomb 2021, p. 250).

4. The Women are Up to Something

Standards of decorum and manners (mores) are sometimes held to be a basic prerequisite for the *emergence* of ethical norms as social lubricants that make complex societies run more smoothly; social mores allow complex societies to flourish as a whole. Unfortunately, however, it is not unusual for norms expressed through evaluatively thick terms to encapsulate properties that undoubtedly contribute to *a group's flourishing*—while at the same time *not contributing to the flourishing of the virtuous agent* who performs the action. Specifically, social mores can simultaneously marginalize and even oppress disadvantaged members of a group. And systematically so. These are precisely the mereological relations—between individual and social circumstances—that infiltrate the fact-value distinction. They also lurk in those thick concepts enshrined in *social norms*—and linguistic usage. What if ethically required behavior does not contribute to the agent's own flourishing? Do such disparities diminish that individual's agency and even their *capacity* to act ethically? Do individual agents structurally disadvantaged by their society's organization have any *moral reason* to adhere to its ethical norms?

The same can be asked of *rituals*. Ritualized practices of religion undoubtedly promote community solidarity. Arguably, however, they also and simultaneously contribute to in-group/out-group distinctions that cause much suffering and disadvantage individuals in the excluded subgroup. Why—*why morally*, that is—should individual agents participate in social rituals if they are personally disadvantaged by them? What moral reasons could be given for requiring individuals to behave morally while further harming themselves? This was an ethical problem Foot explicitly struggled with—and about which she reached no resolution. And yet these questions are central to fictional works like Sophocles' *Antigone*, Ibsen's *Hedda Gabler*, and

Flaubert's *Madame Bovary*. More recently, the well-received novels of James McBride (*The Heaven & Earth Grocery Store*) and Percival Everett (*James*) directly concern relations between a community's social norms and their effects on individuals. And yet fiction is no part of philosophy?

As my comments sprinkled throughout this text suggest, Foot's inability to resolve this issue was in no small part due to the lack of a conceptual framework for non-energetic cause–effect relations. Foot needed a revamped understanding of causal relations (especially of cause-and-effect interactions between the individual and the society to which they belong, in which they are embedded, not just dropped into. The metaphysical terminology with which to rethink a new form of causation as demanded by thick concepts simply did not exist — one that weaves individual actions into social structure such that their cognitive and evaluative framework is embedded and therefore organized by that habitat. The problem with positivism's legacy as an attempt to formulate a science-infused philosophy is that the available science of the day was the wrong science.

Foot's and Murdoch's very different attempts to challenge metaethics gained some traction with the resurgence of virtue ethics towards the end of the twentieth century. Irish-American philosopher Alasdair MacIntyre's *After Virtue* (1981) almost singlehandedly revitalized "the importance of virtue and vice in education and public life" (Lipscomb 2021, p. 239). Twenty years later, the U.S.'s Martha Nussbaum was recognized with the National Humanities Medal for connecting the classical idea of *eudaimonia*, human flourishing, and well-being to the concept of human "capabilities" (*Women and Human Development*, 2000; and *Creating Capabilities: The Human Development Approach*, 2011). Unlike Foot's abstract considerations about those affordances necessary for *human beings in general* to flourish, Nussbaum's capabilities approach drilled down to "what [concrete individuals] are actually able to do and to be" (*Frontiers of Justice*, 2006, p. 70) *given* the circumstances in which they live their lives. She zoomed in to the suite of particular capabilities people living in concrete social conditions require in order to be able to live lives "worthy of the dignity of a human being" (*ibid.*). As Nussbaum takes pains to point out, social justice is about particular affordances and non-affordances that are *not distributed homogeneously* throughout society. Systemic requirements of "human" flourishing and thriving cannot be averaged or considered only in the aggregate: they must be fine-grained to those particular conditions that enable *individuals* entrained within them to flourish. When replying to challenges such as "What do we mean by [Foot's favorite thick concept] rudeness?", identifying the requirements for "human" flourishing in the abstract or at the group level is not enough.

Once conceived from the perspective of the living individuals, the significant role that a community, culture, or state's structure plays in affording, diminishing, stabilizing, and regulating each agent's capabilities comes to the fore. How does a social organization's organization influence its members, actually? How does its structure categorize and treat subgroups and members of those subgroups?

To take context seriously, that is, Nussbaum extended the thick concept of *flourishing* to what it means for the individual, the capabilities afforded or denied him/her as *enabled and maintained — by structural conditions*. The ethical distinction between equality and equity, Nussbaum points out, morally requires nation states to provide conditions that afford each individual's capabilities the capacity to flourish. This demands that we address structural asymmetries in capabilities afforded to privileged and historically excluded members of each community. Internationally, it also means addressing asymmetries in capabilities afforded to residents of unequal and marginalized nations. Nussbaum's capabilities approach demands attention even to asymmetries in cognitive capacities—to remediate those systemic asymmetries that directly impact people with disabilities, for example, and, controversially, even to experimentation on non-human subjects. These same structural features play out differently in different individuals, depending on their unique circumstances and history.

Curiously, although the rise of *virtue ethics* can be attributed in part to Foot's lifelong interest in classical virtues and to Foot's and Anscombe's shared interest in thick concepts. Foot herself did not like the term *virtue ethics*, as Lipscomb points out. She thought it too narrow. Although she maintained that metaethics must be grounded in those "Aristotelian necessities" that human beings need to flourish "and succeed in characteristically human pursuits" (Lipscomb 2021, p. 270), Foot believed that the classical virtues identify only a few of those necessities.

So was Foot willing to countenance any other philosophical methodology other than ordinary language analysis?

I mentioned earlier that Foot's work was better suited to the guild because of her continued adherence to the ordinary language methodology of Oxford philosophy. That commitment, however, raises the question, *who* decides professional norms and methodology; by what criteria are they established? Why analyze only ordinary language declarative statements but not fictional narratives?

Consider the now classic metaethical dilemma that Foot herself invented, the now famous thought experiment on moral decision-making that has since elicited so much discussion in the field of professional ethics that British-

American philosopher Kwame Anthony Appiah labeled it the "trolleyology" cottage industry. Here I am interested not in the content of the thought experiment but the fact that Foot often called her own gedanken-experiment a "useless joke" ("The Problem of Abortion and the Doctrine of Double Effect," 1967). Why? When do acceptable metaphors and thought experiments become unacceptable fables? What (who?) warrants one school of philosophy as determiner of philosophical (or scientific) method *tout court*? It was not until much later in the century that sociology of science became a distinct subfield in philosophy of science; it would keep Popper, Feyerabend, Latour, and Kuhn occupied for years. But not for Foot. For her, the trolley metaphor was no more philosophy than were Murdoch's novels. She had internalized *that* positivist demon and it would not be exorcised.

Anscombe

Anscombe became Wittgenstein's main disciple (his votary, some called her) when his emphasis on "forms of life" "untrapped" her from the limitations of logical positivism. Like Foot's work, Anscombe's primary contribution was therefore squarely within mainstream academic philosophy: she officially secured Wittgenstein's legacy by serving as his primary literary executor. This is not to say that she did not continue to publish in mainstream, peer-reviewed philosophy journals. But not in ethics, as we will see.

Anscombe's interest in thick concepts led her to a different conclusion than Foot's (Anscombe, "Modern Moral Philosophy" — MMP, 1958): Anscombe contended that, like the term "criminal," thick moral concepts such as "right" and "wrong," "ought," "duty," and "obligation" are *meaningful only within a law-based context. Just as no act is criminal in the absence of a law concerning that behavior*, calling something morally right or wrong is meaningless in the absence of a God-like moral lawgiver or its revealed transcription, an Abrahamic Decalogue; the thickness of moral terms presupposes a moral legislator's commands and prohibitions. That legislation and those edicts comprise the empirically determinable matters of fact entangled in the valuational aspect.

But there is no God-like moral giver in a secular, reason-based discipline like philosophy. Therefore, Anscombe concluded, deploying the language of morals in a philosophical (i.e., a secular, agnostic, rationally grounded) context rather than in a faith-based context renders its concepts *thin, no matter how consistently deployed*; in a secular, multicultural society, criteria for attributing qualities like "right" and "good" are uselessly vague and ambiguous.

Moral philosophy is a reflective and rational activity (MMP, 1958)—to that extent and in contrast to emotivism and prescriptivism, Anscombe concluded that there *is* a place for reason in ethics. However, she added, before moral reasoning and moral judgments are even possible, an adequate *philosophy of psychology* (philosophy of mind) is necessary. Even if we are held morally and legally responsible only for intentional behavior, and even if only purposive and "voluntary" actions qualify as morally reprehensible, we can reason about moral value *only* after a sufficiently adequate *moral psychology* has been elaborated. Moral philosophy presupposes a satisfactory moral psychology. And we're not there yet.

Were she alive today Anscombe might still phrase it as follows: we can analyze moral judgments only after cognitive science has satisfactorily explained the empirical facts that underpin psychological perception and intentional causation. At a minimum, moral psychology (philosophy of mind; cognitive science) must account for the empirical ground of meaningful intentionality—how meaningful intentions bring about, inform, and sustain action that achieves its intended purpose. Only after we understand the biology behind the differences between voluntary (like habitual) and involuntary actions—and between intentional and non-intentional (like reflex) behavior—can we engage in moral philosophy. Aristotle's example in the *Nichomachean Ethics* of jettisoning cargo off a boat in a storm remains a live problem for metaethics.

From these considerations, Anscombe concluded that 1) in the absence of a generally agreed-upon moral lawgiver, and 2) until a satisfactory philosophy of mind (aka cognitive science today) is articulated, it is a waste of time to *do* (to study) metaethics. Until the second requirement is satisfied, philosophers should replace common moral predicates like *good* and *right* with *just* and *truthful*. *Just* and *truthful* are more secular and nuanced evaluations that indirectly reference the mental states from which the action was performed, such as judging that a statement can be truthful (when the speaker thought that what they were stating is so) even if the intentional content is factually false. Or that an agent perceives an action as *just* even when it *violates* and was intended to violate existing law.

This radical position explains why most of Anscombe's subsequent publications in professional philosophy journals were almost exclusively devoted to issues surrounding perception and intention, not to moral philosophy *per se*. Squarely situated within analytic philosophy, her articles and books for the most part focused primarily on *intentional* causation, a key issue of philosophical psychology. *What* are intentions and *how* do they bring about and guide behavior such that it is an instance of true agency and therefore action proper—behavior for which the agent can be held morally responsible? Is behavior performed by an individual fitted with prosthetic limbs that are controlled directly by their thoughts a case of intentional causation? These were central concerns of action theory during the last 25 years of the twentieth century. Such questions naturally led to a related topic, our old adversary the problem of causation in general. Are causes in general (and intentional causes—volition?—in particular) necessarily *deterministic* (as causes are expected to be)? Are they only bottom-up, or must philosophy make room for meaningful—that is, top-down—intentional causation of action? How to understand that mechanism?

In a small volume called *Intention* (1957), now something of a minor classic, as well as in "Causality and Determination" (in *Metaphysics and the Philosophy of Mind: Collected Philosophical Papers*, vol. II, 1981b), Anscombe explored philosophical problems that arise when events in the environment (context!) disrupt causal chains, an interest that she shared with her mentor Wittgenstein. In that paper she imagines cases where the flow of information from initial cause to final outcome is interrupted.

Typical *wayward causal chain* narratives in the published literature often went as follows: suppose an agent intends to turn on the light but unbeknownst to her a terrorist has wired the room's electrical circuits so that a bomb goes off when she flips the switch. Bystanders are killed as a result. Did the *agent murder* those bystanders or just *flip* the switch? It is in this sense that philosophers understand the concept of *agency*. Did the person who intentionally flipped the switch in so doing also *culpably* murder those bystanders—as an agent—if they did not intend to murder them? (Note the term *murder* is a thick concept with empirical and moral aspects.)

Illustrating the significance of philosophical psychology, Anscombe follows Aquinas in holding that *intending* an effect is ontologically different from merely *foreseeing* it, as are the moral implications of each of these mental states—as Aristotle's jettisoning cargo in a storm example vividly illustrates. Unlike *agents*, so-called *patients* do not act; they are, as the etymology suggests, passive individuals *to whom* things happen. Their bodily motions do not qualify as action proper, only "mere behavior." Thick moral terms usually point to the presence of intentions. But volitions? As *Dynamics in Action: Intentional Behavior as a Complex System* (1999) was meant to illustrate, I cut my philosophical teeth on these puzzles in action theory. In writing this essay, I am reminded instead of Foot's and Anscombe's rejection of Murdoch's fictional writings. Why did the guild of Anglo-American philosophy—as embodied in Foot's or Anscombe's writings—consider Anscombe's fictional—and, quite frankly, often unrealistic—*wayward causal chains* and Einstein's *gedanken-experiments* acceptable epistemological tools for elucidating truth... but not Murdoch's own fables and novels?

Anscombe clearly understood that the ubiquity of "wayward causal chains" is not limited to intentional causation as in the light switch example. In "Causality and Determination" she draws examples from a wide range of fields, including epidemiology, where the flow of events from initial cause to final outcome is interrupted—where necessary conditions are not sufficient. For instance, individuals who contract infectious diseases can confidently point to their exposure to infected patients as the *cause* of their own illness. But just from knowing that they were exposed to an infected patient they cannot deduce with certainty that they will contract the infection. Other factors might have interrupted the causal chain. The fact that environmental and contextual conditions can indeed disrupt the flow of efficient causes led Anscombe to conclude more generally that causal relationships are not universally determinate.

To phrase it otherwise, Anscombe became a "singularist" about empirical causation (*Stanford Encyclopedia of Philosophy*). Efficient causes are not sufficient because extraneous events can detour a causal sequence; neither do they underwrite universal generalizations. Her conclusion: what are commonly considered empirical *causal laws* are not universal and eternal; they are better reconceptualized as *conditional on context*. To accommodate a wider range of conditions that describe the source (the etiology?) from which an event is "derived," causal relations should be redescribed as "If C then E, *other things being equal.*" In contrast, deriving one thing from another does not require necessitation (*Times, Beginnings, and Causes*, 1981).

Contextual factors that intertwine with particular events and actions can bring about significant effects. Moreover, they do so *not as linear and deterministic efficient causes* but the way herd immunity influences individual incidence. Perhaps we coin thick terms as a short cut that references those mereological distinctions. Had Anscombe made tentative steps in that direction it would have represented a first pass towards a relational ontology, one which her mentor's notion of *forms of life* would have fit into nicely. Specifically, by allowing that systemic contextual factors are real and influence (top-down) those individuals caught up in that context (just not as efficient causes), Anscombe might have taken first steps towards a transformational metaphysics with room for collective forms of life as *having powerful effects* on individuals. Doing so would have acknowledged that contextual embeddedness is not merely epiphenomenal. Such a radical reformulation of the concept of mereological relations would have required a more radical break with the mechanistic notion of causation entrenched at the time.

Anscombe took the first step (rejecting empirical causality as both a sufficient condition and as an instance of an exceptionless lawful generation), but she couldn't quite bring herself to entertain mereology as the answer.

Another fork not taken, but an inevitable one given Kant's earlier decision to bar mereological causes from the realm of the constitutive judgment. My central point here is that Anscombe had no path to a satisfactory notion of causation because she never directly addressed the ontological issue of parts–whole and whole–parts relations. I conclude that, sadly, Anscombe's analytic work on intentional causation was, "better framed for the guild" precisely because she never directly confronted positivism's uncritical reliance on efficient cause-like interactions; the background framework of positivism was too entrenched at the time to be questioned. As a result, and despite her avowed purpose, blurring the fact–value distinction, Anscombe, like Foot and Murdoch, failed to sufficiently advance the project of philosophical psychology with respect to intentional causation such as to provide that ontological foundation on which to build moral philosophy.

The omission allowed the fact–value distinction to remain firmly in place in the halls of Anglo-American philosophy.

Anscombe's handling of the *value side* of the fact–value distinction is even more revealing—and unsettling. If in her own mind a satisfactory philosophy of mind had not yet been properly articulated, what can we say about moral value in the meantime? Her distinction between *causes* and *determinants* suggests that she recognized that contextual nuances must be taken into account in deliberations about causation—both in general and with respect to intentional causation. Why then did she not acknowledge that context must also be implicated in the realm of morality? Anscombe refused to take this fork: her conviction that until philosophical psychology (cognitive science) is fully worked out engaging in moral philosophy is a useless undertaking led her instead to a fateful choice: when moral philosophy must be postponed (until moral psychology is worked out), activism becomes the only option.

Books about the four women all note that Anscombe by and large stopped writing on issues of morality in professional philosophy journals. Instead, she confined her efforts to bring philosophy back to life to public appearances, especially talks and interviews on the BBC. There, her approach turned advocatory, not rationally deliberative and philosophical; she repeatedly refused to critically examine judgments about moral value. In the previous section I argued that this was because she had no way to understand intentional causation as contextually informed and nuanced.

Choosing activism over rational argumentation, especially with respect to moral pronouncements, was unfortunate. The best-known incident of this refusal to reason about moral value is Anscombe's vehement public condemnation and vote, on May 1, 1956, against Oxford University's awarding an honorary degree to Harry Truman. In her testimony, Anscombe insisted that she was not "making a gesture of protest against atomic bombs" because "protests by people who have not power are a waste of time." She was protesting against conferring "honors" on the former president who had ordered the bombings of Hiroshima and Nagasaki; doing so would categorize such actions as "brave" and "just" when the order was in fact morally reprehensible, she maintained. "One can share in the guilt of a bad action by praise and flattery," she testified (quoted in M&W p. 5).

How, exactly, however, do praise and flattery result in (cause? determine?) *sharing* a property with others — whether guilt or any other such quality—when sharing is clearly a relational property? Is this very statement not a foray into moral psychology?

In a pamphlet entitled "Mr. Truman's Degree," Anscombe acknowledged that dropping the two nuclear bombs might have saved more lives than were lost at Hiroshima and Nagasaki. However, and despite recognizing the bombings' empirical *consequences* with respect to "lives going well or badly," she never wavered from the position (the faith?) that calculations about outcomes of actions are irrelevant to moral judgment. Are consequences not to be implicated in thick concepts? It is no coincidence that it was Anscombe who coined the pejorative term *consequentialism* in her 1958 article "Modern Moral Philosophy," notably a work on action theory more than ethics proper. Killing innocents is murder, categorically, regardless of the consequences of not doing so. (Foot's trolleyology thought experiment describes a variant of this same philosophical dilemma.)

Demanding 1) that *all things being equal* clauses be added to cause-effect relations about empirical matters, while simultaneously 2) denying that in the absence of a secular legislator of moral laws current moral concepts are *thick*, led Anscombe to conclude that no empirical consequences or contextual nuances—even if foreseen—can sully the absoluteness of revealed moral imperatives. In her view, no cost-benefit analysis could ever weaken the absolute (because revealed) prohibition against doing "wrongful harm." What do we do about Hare? Well, it seems that in the absence of a fully worked out moral psychology (cognitive science), we retain his universalism but attribute it to revelation, not to mere commitment.

Anscombe might have been a singularist about empirical causal laws, but she was resolutely categorical about moral laws. In her view, moral philosophy would be satisfactory only if its principles are grounded in a general categorical framework (within which those moral judgments are made). And by *law-based* she meant absolute, universal applicability, not the looser causal relations open to *ceteris paribus* qualifications at work in empirical cause–effect interactions. By cleaving the attribution of distinctly *moral* value from *factual* conditions in this way, Anscombe banned any reference to current empirical conditions (much less estimated empirical consequences) in moral reasoning. And since philosophy of mind was in her view still incomplete, she was left with no other recourse than faith, *belief in* divine revelation and scriptures as the sole source of moral value. It is precisely this sharp dichotomy between fact and value that Foot's thick concepts were meant to question.

I can only conclude that, far from being exorcised, Hare remained firmly in place. Anscombe adopted a philosophical stance independent of reasoning—and stuck to it. It was not even a matter of commitment to personal consistency; it was consistency with respect to the Roman Catholic Church's dogma as the only lawgiver of record in her own mind.

I have dwelt on the philosophical details at length to demonstrate that Anscombe's conclusion is not entirely capricious: it is one of several unavoidable consequences of not taking context seriously in all domains. In particular, it means not taking mereological relations seriously, which in turn means not taking seriously constrained interactions and relations that embed individuals in their worlds to create an expanded, smeared-out but coherent and very real dynamic. A context-dependent, relational ontology; not a subjective whimsical idiosyncrasy.

So just as she never agreed with Wittgenstein's views of religion, Anscombe never again questioned Catholic moral teaching after being baptized into the faith. Among her most memorable appearances on the BBC was a vehement defense of Catholic prohibitions against abortion and contraception. Anscombe's reaction upon learning that OXFAM, of which Foot was co-founder and avid promoter, supported contraception? She was simply appalled. Addressing her former colleague (and dear friend) Philippa, Anscombe raged against her on the air for "condoning evil" (Lipscomb 2021, p. 262). No whiff of consequentialist reasoning could sway her. In contrast to her views on empirical cause–effect relations, where she insisted on the need for laws with *ceteris paribus* laws, moral injunctions for Anscombe are categorical and without exceptions. Since an empirically-grounded account of human psychology was still lacking, revealed Catholic dogma offered the only alternative to the arbitrariness of prescriptivism, despite the latter's claims to universalizability.

This position is in stark contrast to the approach Midgley and Murdoch adopted in response to Hare's prescriptivism: for these two, actions undertaken as a result of reflection *can* influence whether our lives go well or badly. In the case of Foot, too, empirically verifiable conditions play a role in those deliberations, as we saw. Ironically, then, especially with regard to Anscombe's stated goal to "do something about Hare," we can only conclude that she simply took a stand and remained consistent with those freely chosen moral principles for the rest of her life. But *why that* stand and not another? Catholic Church teachings overrode everything. For Anscombe, *the pronouncements of that lawgiver* were not open to *rational* deliberation. In the end, Anscombe's position in effect left Hare's prescriptivism firmly in place.

Such consequences of not taking context seriously in morality and public life are still with us today.

Despite their run-in over OXFAM's support of contraception, on a BBC talk after Anscombe's death Foot publicly praised Anscombe for her "devotion to truth." One can only wonder if Foot's particular choice of words was meant to imply that Anscombe's devotion to "truth" was limited to the fact side of the fact–value distinction.

Midgley

And what about Midgley? Midgley's contribution to Lipscomb's query — "What came of it all?" — was that it was Midgley who "connected the idea of human flourishing to an updated account of the animals we are" (Lipscomb 2021, p. 238). As we shall see, the ethological and ecological lens through which she came to view the fact–value distinction blurred it even more effectively than Foot's thick concepts. Indeed, it wasn't so much a lens as a zoom-out dial. Indirectly, a wider ecological perspective foregrounded the issue of mereological relations. Midgley folded biology and "culture" into each other as well as into the very core of the features of a rich human life. However, because her writings and media appearances were pitched to a broader audience than just "the guild" of professional philosophers, it took decades for her to be recognized as a philosopher at all — despite arguably having inspired what is now called *Environmental Ethics*.

She was fortunate to live long enough to witness it.

Mary Scrutton (as she was before marriage) remained in the civil service until Fall of 1947 when she returned to Oxford to do graduate research. In remarks about the pros and cons of postgraduate studies, she often noted her growing disaffection at the time with academia: while it "shows you how to deal with difficult arguments," it does not "help you to grasp the big questions that provide its context—the background issues out of which the small problems arose." Midgley, who never completed her PhD, wrote that she was "lucky" to have missed out on obtaining a doctorate by accepting a position teaching philosophy at Reading University (1949–1951).

After her 1950 marriage to Geoffrey Midgley, who had accepted a philosophical position at Newcastle University, the couple moved to that city; Mary stopped teaching and put her career on hold while their three sons were young. Living first in Reading and then in Newcastle (universities the Oxbridge crowd disparagingly labeled "red brick colleges") gave her space to explore the "background" context from which "small problems arose." She began to notice, for example, that paradoxes appear not only in formal axiomatic systems as Russell and Gödel had realized (M&W p. 262); they also show up in real life, including in daily language. Rather than considering them logical puzzles, Midgley described paradoxes as the philosophical equivalent of plumber's work: they uncover flaws in a pipe that let water leak out—but the flaw itself also lets the light in. They are instructive; they expose flaws in ordinary thinking. Midgley often commented that paradoxes are also useful to social reformers; they foreground anomalies and contradictions between what we ordinarily say and what we actually do. (Incidentally, the plumber metaphor was favored by Philippa as well as Mary, which would be unsurprising were it not for Foot's kneejerk dismissal of fables and tales.)

The influence of informal analysis began to wane; ordinary thinking, too, can be mistaken. But a wider lens can disambiguate the problem. As can a pragmatism-informed perspective.

Unemployed at first in Newcastle, Midgley gave talks on these topics on the BBC, many of which were broadcast as book discussions. The subjects she covered were wide-ranging. Noticing and paying attention to her surroundings (not just to linguistic terminology) played a vital role in her thinking. As a stay-at-home married woman with three young children, she talked on air about questions she asked herself about the place of women in society (M&W p. 268). One early fact she noticed was that published philosophical works on the "rights of man" and "man's nature" were invariably centered on the role of *men* — in politics, law, commerce, and education — not the rights of all of human-kind, but the rights of *males*. During one radio appearance she presented the interviewer with a list she had compiled of famous philosophers. The list showed that practically all were not only male; they were also *bachelors* (*ibid.*, p. 269; https://ravenmagazine.org/magazine/rings-books/)! Only Socrates, Aristotle, and Hegel were married. Because of his serial philandering, Rousseau did not qualify!

Midgley's point, of course, was that this is not a random coincidence: the social condition of bachelorhood affords the luxury to concentrate and think uninterruptedly for long stretches of time. Thanks to a female-provided support infrastructure, male philosophers had the time and leisure to reflect on issues about rights in the abstract, without interference from household or marital obligations — without interference from the everyday context of a well-rounded human life, that is. I always thought the same about Thoreau: easy to wax rhapsodic about bucolic life when your mother continues to do your laundry and packs you baked meals to take back to your cabin in the woods.

When considered in the light of the wider human context, Midgley added, many philosophical questions and their traditional answers can similarly be put into doubt. In an interview late in life she remarked, for example, that no one with an infant suckling at the breast would ever think to question the reality of "other minds": the mother knows exactly what the baby is feeling and why—the baby is fussing because of the spicy food the mother ate for lunch a few hours ago, which is giving her an upset stomach as well! Leibniz's identity of indiscernibles, another commonly accepted philosophical principle, likewise appears in a different light when discussed in the context of pregnancy, where, arguably, two individuals are in the same place at the same time. And on and on. The identity of nested individuals is a core question in mereology.

In 1952, shortly after moving to Newcastle, and on the recommendation of her father, Midgley picked up a newly translated book by Nobel Prize winning ethologist Konrad Lorenz at the local bookstore. She had always been interested in nature; as a child she collected newts rather than dolls. On more than one occasion Midgley reported that, before reading Lorenz, she had not realized that the term *animal* groups together diverse creatures into one "abstract collective *so that they could be contrasted with humans*" (M&W p. 277, my emphasis): the classification, she concluded, just lets humans know "I am one of Nature's little kings" qualitatively distinct from the rest of the creatures. In reality, as she goes on to point out, careful study reveals that the opposition is nothing but a human construct. "Our lives are animal lives are in many ways continuous with those of fleas, gorillas..." (*ibid.*, p. 278). This sudden insight that there is no [real] opposition between animal and human was an integrative flash of insight [to] an interspecies collective, a "mixed community" (*ibid.*, p. 278).

It changed her philosophical outlook.

From that moment on the newfound ecological lens allowed Midgley to pursue her lifelong interest in nature; it deepened her understanding of the biological foundations of (animal) behavior, and most importantly for our purposes it pointed the way to a renewed and expanded concept of human beings and their environment, as more coherent, and ecological (that is, systemic) unities integrated into our surroundings and even our past. This new perspective was not a change of direction; it enlarged the context in which her earlier philosophical ideas were situated. Midgley often noted, for instance, that unlike existentialists, both Thomists and Marxists find an intelligible unity of man and nature. For *intelligible*, I submit, read *rationally tractable*. Furthermore, the structure and pattern of that unity are not only essential to value; they are also a source of wonder (M&W p. 238). So, if it is to have any hope of explaining the multidimensional and context-dependent necessities humans require to flourish and thereby provide a more satisfactory understanding of fact, value, agency, and the rest of these "wicked problems," philosophy must fold into its conceptual apparatus the full panoply of contextual conditions that envelop human beings, including those cultural/symbolic dimensions as well as well those of their biological heritage.

In other words, Midgley recognized that to explain how such unities are generated and maintained—at every dimension of reality—philosophy must rethink ontology relationally and contextually. She took her time; she was 59 years old when she published the first of her nineteen books.

But it paid off.

With respect to morality even Anscombe had recognized that "Wickedness is not a character-trait... it means intentionally doing acts that are wrong" (MMP, 1958). "The background to our lives can, if badly arranged, make wicked acts quite easy for quite ordinary and friendly people. Given the right circumstances, 'a quite mediocre person can do spectacularly wicked things'" (from "Mr. Truman's Degree,"

1957). In light of that acknowledgement, why then did Anscombe refuse to question Church teaching? I submit that "background [presuppositions] to our [moral] lives" are as easy to take for granted and ignore as background context that turns flipping a switch into a terrorist act. Perhaps being a female outsider in a red brick college gave her a perspective on context that the others lacked. In contrast to Anscombe, and to Midgley's credit, the ecological lens led her to explicitly renounce "essentialism" and the notion that character traits are exclusively internal.

More deeply than the other three, Midgley faced this issue head-on and reconceptualized the category "human" to encompass physical, biological, as well as sociocultural niches—the overall milieu—which interacting individual organisms and environments co-create and in which they are entangled. Scientists today call these local and temporal synergies "soft assemblies." With respect to human social organization, they constitute Wittgenstein's *forms of life*. Analogous to ecological habitats, they consist of concrete, intertwined, and interlocking interdependencies that define unique dynamics for each individual as well as for the group. Because that background is intertwined into the cognitive and affective dynamics of individual human beings, whether it is a well- or poorly-arranged background (read structure, habitat, niche, family, or state) is as central to a person's concrete actions as requiring that that agent act intentionally is. How does the distributed "intentionality" of a complex system exercise agency?

Unlike her three friends, Midgley studied humans in their full dimensionality. Doing so rearranged the moral landscape as fundamentally as ecosystems reorganize the possibility space of living things; it cut the ethical world at a different set of joints (the joints of a now more comprehensive fact/axiology complex): "beasts" are not exclusively "beastly," and human beings are "animals" too. This insight blurred the boundaries between individual organisms and the biological niches, habitats, ecosystems, social organizations, and cultures in which they are embedded. Divvying up reality into relational and interdependent equivalence classes recognizes the reality of *worlds*, of *umwelts*. Phrased otherwise, thanks to ongoing feedback loops, an individual organism's properties and actions extrude into and alter the niche in which it lives just as much as features of the niche or habitat—or *umwelt*—become integrated into the individual organism's defining constraint regime. Causality goes bottom-up as well as top-down, morally as well as empirically, to create a cohesive, multidimensional whole. We call this overall process of fitting together *natural selection*. By integrating context-dependent functionalities into the specimen's personal properties, the newly drawn complex thereby blurs the sharp distinction between fact and value. It values fact and factualizes value. As Allen *et al.* (1984, 1982) note, integration through feedback can create a control system that regulates and modulates components in terms of a *preferred range of states*. The viable and sustainable range of states that support a flourishing system comprises the values and norms (the set points) of that control system. As relations in social organizations become increasingly complex, some of those norms represent moral values.

Since all human beings are equally primates, mammals, vertebrates, etc., Midgley's biological approach echoed Aristotle's understanding of the Virtues: look inside the *biological aspect* of any organism for its fundamental nature. In contrast to Aristotle, however, today's twist as revealed by the study of mutualisms and epigenetics—of context-dependent complex systems in general—is that key features of the *inside* are not independent of the *outside*: they cannot stand alone independent of the environment—key features of the current phenotype are not products of the genome alone. The "nature" of living things is now understood to be much more than just primary qualities; our nature is in effect a smeared-out mutualism that is fully context-dependent and historical. The properties in question include spatio-temporally-conditioned traits inherited from the context in which the organism's progenitors lived. The current *inside* milieu is interdependent with and conditioned on *past environments*. And critically, *present* insides also anticipate and thus bias *which* of the range of outside *futures* is most likely to be realized (Robert Rosen 1991). The study of epigenetics and holobionts amply confirms this claim. An integrative, synthetic, and diachronic dynamic embodies the conditions organisms need to flourish—and to fully exercise their agency so as to adapt and evolve in light of changing conditions—at every level of organization and at any moment in time. Determining the "nature" of particular animals—as a mammal, member of the species *Homo sapiens*, etc.—specifies the "necessities" each individual here and now needs to flourish.

As unremarkable as these sentences sound today, such ecology-infused language would have struck academic philosophers (especially during Midgley's early years as a philosophy professor at Newcastle) more like cultural anthropology or social psychology than philosophy. It is unsurprising, therefore, that just as they had dismissed the philosophical reflections in Murdoch's fictional works from the domain of "proper philosophy," Anscombe and Foot once again disapproved of Midgley's efforts to bring biology to bear in discussions about the conditions for human flourishing. Foot never did understand what Midgley was up to with her deliberately multidisciplinary approach to moral philosophy. Biology? What *is* she thinking? As she had done with Murdoch, Foot henceforth relegated Midgley to the margins of academia because of it.

With the benefit of hindsight, however, we can safely declare that if Foot is hailed as the progenitor of virtue ethics, and Anscombe as godmother of mid-twentieth-century action theory, enlarging the category of value to incorporate the biological resources all living things need to flourish has secured Midgley's legacy as a foundational reference for *environmental ethics*. The more recent 4E *approach* to the subjects of agency and action also owes much to these four women's attempts to bridge the fact–value distinction. Of the four metaphysicals, however, it was Midgley who took the most concrete steps towards integrating facts and values by bringing together the enabling and governing constraints the two concepts share. Causal influences in complex dynamical systems go both ways, from parts to whole and back. Midgley's answer to "What do we do with Hare?" was to zoom out to an ecological perspective and, by analogy, demonstrate how ethical values reflect the interdependent constraints from which they emerge.

Alas, however, Midgley too had internalized the Oxfordian philosophical presuppositions of the times. Despite how fundamentally the new field of ethology (founded by Lorenz and whom Midgley came to know personally) influenced her reasoning, like the others, she never directly challenged the presuppositions about causality that were central to the positivist worldview; specifically, she never proposed an alternative meta-theoretical account of mereological relations—the causal relations between individual specimens and ecological niche, habitat, and especially psychosocial organization and culture they inhabit. The positivist paradigm was just too entrenched.

Blame it on the fact that the terminology and concepts subtending this complementary worldview had not yet been formulated. That there was no metaphysical framework within which to think about ontological coherence-making, the prohibition against circular causality made the ideas of self-integration and self-constraint even less fathomable. Analysis was all the rage, as were siloed and rigidly bounded categories.

Synthesis? Mutualism and symbiosis? Not so much.

Today, iterated and recursive processes play a central role in artificial intelligence; the output of one run is fed back into the initial and boundary conditions of the next. We know now that such feedback loops can produce remarkably unexpected systemwide order. But limited exclusively to explanations formulated in terms of deterministic forceful causes, mainstream Anglo-American philosophy lacked any framework for that spiral "form of causality unknown to us" which Kant had identified but which remained as yet unexplained. Until the relatively recent discovery of autocatalytic sets (Kauffman 1993), the notion of "constraint closure" (Montevil and Mossio 2015), and the development of neural networks trained on recursive backprop algorithms, professional philosophers still lacked such a language and the discipline remained encapsulated in very positivist boundaries.

That said, however, Midgley might have nonetheless inadvertently opened a door with a remark to the effect that *animals resolve conflict not through logical deduction but by myriad adjustments in their behavior. "Reason… is a name for organizing oneself,"* she states. What causative mechanisms embody ongoing adjustments in behavior and properties such as to produce a resilient and robust metastable dynamic? Redefining rationality—and *a fortiori* reasoning and sense-making to include multiple constraint satisfaction as a form of causality—reframes the very meaning of cognition and rational relations, perhaps even the concept of information. Despite writing "from the margins of the discipline," where philosophy overlapped with biology, Midgley was among the first to present a positive proposal for the kind of moral philosophy compatible with "a naturalistic ecological ontology, grounded in the character and needs of the human animal." More generally, Midgley proposed *an ethics of self-integration*, of thinking through how to do justice to our whole selves (Lipscomb 2021, p. 233) and the world which we co-create and which we inhabit. This is not a "take a stand, any stand" theory because empirical conditions will affect how effective we are at doing so. We ignore that spatiotemporal context at our peril.

Perhaps Spinoza's *conatus*, the innate inclination of things, is not just a "striving to persevere in its being." Perhaps it is better conceptualized as a universal tendency to produce patterns of integrated metastability. Integration into an organized and novel form of Becoming (into a new constraint regime) is at the same time the creation of (relational) information. It is what nature does well, and routinely. The universe's *conatus* might therefore be a pervasive tendency to a form of *becoming* that gives pre-eminence to active coherence-making. If complexity theory is correct, it is also a tendency in conformity with the second law of thermodynamics as it plays out in open systems far from equilibrium.

Alas, for much of Midgley's life, professional philosophers marginalized her ethological and ecological observations as irrelevant to the discipline. The philosophical significance of her oeuvre is only now being recognized.

Conclusion

The positivist mindset entrenched in the North Atlantic academy after WWII prevented the four women—who were indeed *on* to the right approach—from fully reaching their avowed goal of "doing something about Hare." The conviction that philosophy is *only* "done" the way it is "done at Oxford" drove two of them out of academic philosophy: Murdoch and Midgley left to write fiction and work in biology, respectively—and for decades were relegated to the margins of philosophy.

Murdoch's resignation from Oxford allowed her to explore a wide range of directions in works of fiction where she could more freely examine the multidimensional human condition. Murdoch's rich contextual novelistic descriptions of commonplace human dilemmas delved into the moral problems encountered in daily life. As I wryly remarked in *Dynamics in Action*: to plumb the richness of human life and behavior Balzac and Proust will always trump Hempel and Oppenheim. Alas, Murdoch was never able to shrug off the belief that authoring richly descriptive and reflective novels just did not count as "doing philosophy"—proper Oxford philosophy, that is.

In contrast, Foot and Anscombe chose to remain officially within Anglo-American philosophy's accepted manual of style. But as demonstrated earlier, Anscombe could not get past the fact–value distinction—not even after flaws in the Newtonian understanding of causation became apparent to her. In her writings, fact and value remained disjoined, and interrupted efficient causal chains wreaked havoc on lawful predictions. So she never again published professionally on ethics and public policy. She chose instead to live in two non-overlapping realms: professionally respectable and publish-worthy writing on intentional causation and action on the one hand, and activism through public lectures and testimonies on the other.

For her part, Foot did not fully analyze the type of causation that links individually virtuous actions on the one hand to collectively fashioned social norms and practices on the other. As described earlier, Foot was well aware that although these might systemically allow communities to flourish, they simultaneously disadvantage some individuals. A satisfactory resolution of this tension would have required her to explore the emergence of mereological relations from which systemic values and norms arise. Perhaps it was precisely because she was so intent on remaining within the guild, but whatever the reason Foot never pursued the path towards which "thick concepts" pointed: towards a context-informed metatheory. She just could not take that extra step—just as she never quite fathomed what Midgley was doing rooting around in biology.

So, in the end, it was left to Mary Midgley, the longest lived, to carry the banner of "bringing philosophy back to life." Literally, back to biology. The requirements for a flourishing life, she showed, are multidimensional: they are social, cognitive, and affective—and biological. It took a while for philosophy to begin paying attention. Even today, folding in ecological and evolutionary—that is, richly contextual—considerations into philosophy is perhaps the most fruitful way of getting at the complex intertwining of hierarchical and heterarchical forms of biopsychosocial organization, and of showing how such complex dynamics *integrate* the two aspects of the old fact-value distinction.

But, to repeat, understanding those spatiotemporal interdependencies requires a complementary metaphysics of causation. And mainstream North Atlantic philosophy today has still not fully accepted that bringing philosophy back to life means more than understanding language usage in light of "forms of life." It means also returning natural, perspectival, and social contexts to metaphysics as well as epistemology. Even complexity theorists were hard pressed to formulate meta-theoretical accounts of these interwoven relations. The epistemological turn that Kant initiated over 125 years ago must now be supplemented with a dynamical and contextual turn in metaphysics; it is only just now getting off the ground in neuroscience. With respect to epistemology, it demands a thorough rethinking of social psychology, of the context-dependent aspects of reason beyond bare deduction and how cognition manifests across nested contexts. (I have suggested elsewhere that a form of multiple constraint satisfaction is involved.)

Ontologically, it demands a thorough revamping of the concept of causation generally, and of recursive causality in particular. And how hierarchy- (coherence-) formation emerges as a result. How, in reality, "externalities" are often not external *tout court* and consequently must be brought back into metatheory. Conversely, how some "internalities" extrude into the environment and effectively change it. Metatheory must capture those smeared out realities and ecological epistemology must provide an account of perception that does not violate the principles of physics.

But for most of the twentieth century this sort of approach was branded as "continental philosophy"—and dismissed. In view of a dominant conceptual framework that relied exclusively on efficient cause and on internal primary properties as the locus of *essence* and *identity*, the Academy closed itself off to the very possibility of mereology. Academics simply had no concepts with which to conceive of relational, synthetic, and processual causal relations; they had no language in which to articulate the systemic interdependencies and mutualist influences that happen in open, far from equilibrium conditions. *That* is why the theoretical framework philosophers adopted from modern physics had no choice but to consider epiphenomenal those interactions between individual entities (living or nonliving) and the wider context in which they exist. As a result, twentieth-century philosophers had no alternative but to maintain that things that *appear* to be coherent wholes (like organisms) are in fact ultimately reducible to isolated particles careening about within a closed featureless space in response to forceful impacts. In time, all the jostling about was presupposed to settle down into a final and homogeneous thermal state of white noise, the heat death of the universe.

That was the dominant picture of the universe in Anglo-American university philosophy departments—until quite recently, when nonlinear accounts of far from equilibrium thermodynamics began to shake up the existing conceptual landscape with innovative ideas like *complex attractors* and *fractals* and a new theoretical framework with which to inform the models. Until now, however, the notion of coherent and integrative totalities arising from processes other than efficient causes got shoved back into the closet of philosophy and natural science for another century.

Remarkable as their achievements were, we can now appreciate that the influence of these four remarkable women was hindered by an entrenched professional paradigm that dominated the period and for decades after—and which they had internalized. Their story recapitulates missed opportunities to synthesize a contextually nuanced metaphysics and epistemology once and for all. By laying bare this sedimented history this monograph has attempted to clear the trailhead of debris that prevents us from seeing the path that takes context seriously.

Appendix

Demonstrating that purely physical and chemical flows self-organize into complex systems called *dissipative structures* earned Ilya Prigogine the 1977 Nobel Prize in Chemistry. These systems reach and maintain a form of metastability that is qualitatively different from the heat death equilibrium of classical thermodynamics. Far from violating the second law, dissipative structures formed in open conditions far from equilibrium satisfy that law, even as the ongoing structural order they create delays the final state of thermal equilibrium. Physical processes such as cosmogenesis, Bénard cells, whirlpools, some biochemical reactions, the biosphere, ecosystems, and even living things, human beings, and their social organizations are all enacted in two-way flows of matter, energy, and information. Significantly, these systems not only display distinct emergent properties that cannot be fully derived solely from those of their components; they also control—top-down—those components such that they persist as coherent wholes.

But an ontology of separate, homogeneous particles pushed about solely by energetic forces cannot account for how novel and active synthesis, coherence, symbiosis, synergy, and mutualism arise and persist in the face of the second law (Juarrero 2023). The frosty reception of Lynn

Margulis's demonstration of symbiosis shows that in more than a century after Darwin attitudes had not changed that much since the heyday of positivism. An alternative approach might sound something like this: emergent systemic dynamics are the outcome of constrained interactions among individual entities in far from equilibrium conditions, conditions which are themselves the outcome of *constraints*. Circular and spiral relations brought about by the workings of constraints are at the heart of the natural formation of *heterarchies* (collectives in which no component or level of organization is either uppermost or dominates the rest).

We can begin with the uncontroversial assumption that nothing comes from randomness. Complexification cannot happen in conditions of white noise. Following the lead of Lila Gatlin (1964), Juarrero (1999 and 2023) speculated that some form of *context-independent constraints* precipitated the Big Bang and cosmic inflation. *Context-independent constraints (CICs) take conditions away from equilibrium or equiprobability.* The Big Bang, cosmic inflation, and the formation of light elements are primordial symmetry breaks of this sort; viewed through the lens of complexity theory, CICs established the earliest inhomogeneities that became manifest as spacetime. Molecular chirality (handedness), spin, gradients of density, polarity, charge, pressure, temperature are evidence of other CICs in the early universe; these features are context-independent prerequisites for the formation of more complex systems. They differentiate more or less local, more or less persistent, spatial and temporal areas of spacetime across a variety of dimensions and scales. Each new inhomogeneity sets up potential for further differentiation — into individual heavy elements as well as stars and galaxies, for starters.

Context-independent constraints alone cannot have gotten us from the Big Bang to today's complex universe. Why didn't the nascent cosmos centrifugally dissipate into nothingness as per the second law? Or conversely, given the warping of spacetime we call gravity, why did it not centripetally collapse into a massive black hole? Nonuniform conditions (perhaps density of matter in stars, or thermal gradients deep underwater) might have coincided by chance such that at various thresholds of instability a different sort of constraint, *context-dependent constraints* (CDCs), appeared. Might the Pauli exclusion principle be an early CDC?

Bottom-Up Integration into Interdependent Wholes

CDCs take *conditions far from independence*. Examples include feedback, recursion, timing, ordinality, iteration, catalysis, and especially autocatalytic conformation (Kauffman 1993). *Bottom-up* they link erstwhile independent entities or processes into greater wholes with emergent properties that can persist despite continuous turnover of their actual components. Heterarchies form. CDCs are therefore *enabling constraints* that integrate individual events and things into new syntheses with novel qualities such as synchrony and synergy. In turn, these emergents can be embodied as waves even as they simultaneously establish yet another inhomogeneity in the cosmos. Coherence-making thus extends the interdependence of constraints to the context from which it arose. Molecules, slime molds, living things, and the biosphere are other instances of this dynamic—as are social organisms. Because the qualitatively novel emergent dynamics satisfy the second law they can sustain and persist despite turnover and replacement of their components.

Complex structures of process are therefore collective dynamics generated in response to context-*dependent* constraints working against a background of context-*independent* constraints. Phrased otherwise, syntheses and synergies are, ontologically, enveloping and overarching *constraint regimes*; they are order parameters of integrated—interlocking and interdependent—constraints (Juarrero 2023). Complex systems in this sense are dynamics whose integration manifests systemwide and qualitatively novel properties that are not reducible to the sum of its components (*ibid.*). The possibility of creative cosmic and biological evolution is predicated on these dynamics.

CDCs and the greater wholes whose formation they facilitate can be spatial or temporal. Examples of novel qualities that emerge from *enabling spatial* CDCs include the appearance of *functional* properties. 3D protein structures are formed in response to spatial constraints on 2D amino acid chains. Genetically identical rabbits grow white fur at high altitudes but brown fur at sea level. Setting up the bauplan during embryogenesis relies on spatial constraints to express the proper phylogenetic information; the process is not specified in the genome.

Examples of *temporal enabling CDCs* include timing and ordinality (position in a series). Perhaps Heisenberg matrices capture the earliest appearance of ordinality? Temporal CDCs' constraints determine integral sequences that manifest novel emergent properties (see Heinrich 2018). Dissipative structures are historical; they record in their very dynamic the temporal and spatial constraints under which they were created. Such *path-dependence* is a form of primordial memory. Migrating birds are defined by their present attunement to seasonal changes in ambient light in response to natural selection. We call the process of inheritable CDCs *epigenetics*. In epigenetic processes, spatiotemporal context qualitatively alters things and events without violating causal closure or requiring changes in an organism's genome. Significantly, contextual constraints are not causal in virtue of energy transfer.

Ilya Prigogine's work on the formation of dissipative structures illustrates how such spatiotemporal heterarchy formation comes about. Examples include the transition from conduction to convection (Bénard) cells. Here, water and other viscous fluids subject to contextual constraints (a pan of water uniformly heated from below) self-organize into macroscopic, hexagonal, 3D rolling columns of liquid. Such structures of process create information by adding degrees of freedom to the possibility landscape. Another example of dissipative structures is the transformation of colorless drops of chemicals into the colorful, macroscopic waveforms discovered by Belousov-Zhabotinsky. The key insight considered worthy of Nobel Prize recognition was that the "creation of order out of chaos" in this manner satisfies the second law. So does the origin of life.

The general principle is the following: under open, far-from equilibrium conditions (a critical difference with classical, near equilibrium thermodynamics), unlikely perturbations or fluctuations at thresholds of instability (tipping points) can become amplified by *positive feedback*. "Amplified by context" means that context-dependent constraints entrain previously isolated entities into new macroscopic collectives, a qualitatively distinct dynamic. Amplification thus precipitates a phase transformation into a new form of order: water flow becomes "turbulence" and whirlpools form. Synergies and mutualisms generated in this manner qualitatively alter the possibility landscape into a new topology with distinct *order parameters*. Such parametrized space constitutes the appearance of a *constraint regime* (Juarrero 2023). Juarrero (*ibid.*) proposed that this dynamic is found in the biotic and psychosocial realms as well.

Constraint Regimes as Constitutive of a New Form of Order

Once entrained into a convection cell or a BZ waveform in this manner, the behavior of the water or chemical molecules is *governed* by the order parameter of the new pattern. By "entrained" I mean that the behavior of each molecule is now controlled, top-down, by the overarching attractor within which it was captured—be that a rolling column of fluids or a translational colorful waveform. Or species in an ecosystem. Enveloping *constraint regimes* become the *constitutive constraints* of new dynamics. They signal an emergent and enveloping level of a novel heterarchical organization.

To repeat, emergent properties generally are neither new material stuff nor the direct consequences of energy transfer; they are embodied in novel *order parameters*. Consider homeostasis, a pre-eminent constraint regime. The term describes the continuous and mutually constrained adjustments of digestive, endocrinological, neurological, and other physiological processes to maintain an organism's health and viability. This balancing act is implemented as an ongoing negative feedback mechanism that selectively *adjusts the range of* values of the components' properties and behaviors such that the health and viability (the emergent property of its constraint regime) are maintained (*ibid.*). Top-down causation in this sense is a selective process. The controlling level of organization—the homeostatic constraint regime—is not reducible because "range of values to preserve viability or health" is not new material stuff; it is a set of relational, path-dependent and interlocking, interdependent constraints—radically contextually so.

Constitutive Constraints Acting as Governing Constraints

More generally: *top-down control* by constraint (Juarrero 1998) is possible only because constitutive and strongly emergent constraint regimes become *second-order, context-dependent governing constraints* on their components—all within the background of the extant context-independent landscape (*ibid.*) in which they exist. Top-down causation in this sense is implemented in cascades of *mutual constraint satisfaction* across multiple dimensions and scales. Acting as a governing *negative feedback* mechanism, second-order governing constraints regulate, modify, and otherwise guide and shape components, their configurations, and their behavior such that the order parameters of the overarching constraint regime hold.

Top-down causation (from emergent property's order parameters to constituents) is possible only because constraint regimes are persistent. Unlike frozen water molecules, the dissipative dynamics of whirlpools and convection cells can persist far from equilibrium despite turnover of individual components and perturbations from the environment. Persistence, in turn, presupposes *metastability* (see Juarrero 2023, Chapter 15). And notably, metastability is possible only because constraint regimes self-organized in this manner are *multiply realizable*: the same emergent property describable as a biological function can be realized in a variety of different processes. Conversely (because of their path-dependence), complex systems are also often *degenerate*: the same micro process might actualize different higher-level functions if entrained in a different attractor. As a bonus, this *historicity* (path-dependence) *makes* multiply realizable complex systems responsive to changing local conditions.

Persistence, metastability, multiple realizability, and historicity must all be "cashed out" in terms of thermodynamics. The metastability and multiple realizability of complex systems are themselves the outcomes of thermodynamic coherence-making by constraint; they are features that arise as the result of the very processual interdependence that constitutes and defines the new constraint regime. This is the twenty-first century's understanding of strong emergence and mereological top-down causation.

In summary, complexity theory developed in the last fifty years provides a model with which to rethink synthesis and integration, not simply as epistemological tools, but as ontological processes. The formation of integral totalities with components is, ontologically, the natural bottom-up generation of overarching novel constitutive constraint regimes that govern (control) their components through cascades of top-down second-order constraints — all without fusing the components into an undifferentiated mass. Coherence-formation viewed through the lens of complex dynamical systems theory signals the formation of context-dependent *heterarchies* with lines of influence both bottom-up from parts to whole and top-down from whole to components. And horizontally at the same heterarchical level of organization.

With the addition of the concept of *enabling* and *constitutive/governing* constraints, I believe that complex dynamical systems theory can account for the real formation of interdependent and mutualist heterarchical dynamics. It can also *explain* both bottom-up and top-down interlevel relations—micro constraints among constituents generating wholes bottom-up, and systemic, top-down constraints regulating micro processes such that the emergent qualities (functionality, viability) persist. This includes the interlevel relations between individuals and the systemic whole to which they belong. It also explains the dynamic of embedding in and interdependence with context generally, which CDCs turn into an enveloping level of governing and regulatory order. Over time, creative evolution thus becomes possible.

The flexibility and generative potential for adaptation and evolution that this integrative propensity adds to the "furniture" of the cosmos cannot be underestimated. Incorporating context-dependent dynamics against a background of context-independent constraints closes a figure-eight loop of processes and constraints that is extended in space and time. It is a "strange loop" that goes from linking previously *isolated* entities bottom-up, into an ecology of *interdependent* mutualist processes, embedded in the context that enabled the heterarchy to form—and then *from* the overarching constitutive constraint regime top-down *to* control and regulate its components such that its overall metastability is maintained.

Lacking a metaphysics of synthetic causation made top-down causation a controversial philosophical topic for centuries. Indeed, it made the whole issue intractable. As this work has shown, it led Anglo-American philosophy to a dead end by entrenching positivism as its sole paradigm. The promise of this Appendix is that complex dynamical systems theory offers a way to understand mereological relations in terms of formation and control by constraint in such a way as to make parts-to-whole and whole-to-parts relations tractable—all without violating principles of causal closure and conservation of mass and energy. Related philosophical controversies about the reality of "structural" influences on individuals; criteria of personal identity; and especially relations between mental processes and physical ones can now be understood from a richer perspective.

We pay for this cosmic tendency to synthesize and integrate by giving up strict determinism and certainty.

It is worth the price.

References

Allen, T.F.H., R.V. O'Neill, and T.W. Hoekstra 1984. Interlevel Relations in Ecological Research and Management: Some Working Principle from Hiearchy Theory. *USDA Forest Service General Technical Report RM-110.* pp. 1–12.

Allen, T.F.H., and T.B. Starr. 1982. First edition. *Hierarchy.* University of Chicago Press.

Anderson, P.W., 1972. More is different. *Science* 177, no. 4047: 393–396.

Anscombe, G.E.M., 1957. *Intention.* Basil Blackwell.

Anscombe, G.E.M., 1956. "Mr. Truman's Degree" [Online] https://faculty.uca.edu/rnovy/Anscombe--Mr%20Truman%27s%20Degree%202.htm

Anscombe, G.E.M., 1958. "Modern Moral Philosophy," *Philosophy* 33, no. 124: 1–16.

Anscombe, G.E.M., 1971. *Causality and Determination: An Inaugural Lecture.* Cambridge University Press.

Anscombe, G.E.M., 1975. *Times, Beginnings, and Causes.* Oxford University Press.

Artigiani, Robert, 2023. "Shifting Paradigms: Beyond Modern Science to Complexity and Ethics" (Fall 2023) *Northern Prairies Ethics Journal* vol. IX: 1–98.

Ayer, A.J., 1936. *Language, Truth, and Logic.* Dover.

Ball, Philip, 2023. *How Life Works: A User's Guide to the New Biology.* University of Chicago Press.

Bergson, Henri, 1911. *Creative Evolution* (trans into English). Henry Holt and Company.

Brentano, Franz, 1884. "Intentionality." In *Psychology from an Empirical Standpoint*. Routledge.

Cockett, Richard, 2023. *Vienna: How the City of Ideas Created the Modern World*. Yale University Press.

Egginton, William, 2023. *The Rigor of Angels: Borges, Heisenberg, Kant, and the Ultimate Nature of Reality*. Pantheon.

Foot, Philippa, 1967. "The Problem of Abortion and the Doctrine of Double Effect." *Oxford Review* 5: 1–5.

Foot, Philippa, 1959. "Moral Beliefs." *Proceedings of the Aristotelian Society* vol. 59, no. 1: 83–104.

Foot, Philippa, 1958. "Moral Arguments." *Mind* vol 67, no 268: 502–513.

Frank, Adam, M. Gleiser and E. Thompson, 2024. *The Blind Spot: Why Science Cannot Ignore Human Experience*. MIT Press.

Gillett, Carl, 2016. *Reduction and Emergence in Science and Philosophy*. Cambridge University Press.

Hare, R.M., 1952. *Language of Morals*. Oxford University Press.

Heinrich, J. 2018. *The Secret of Our Success*. Princeton University Press.

Juarrero, Alicia, 2023. *Context Changes Everything: How Constraints Create Coherence*. MIT Press.

Juarrero, Alicia, 2013. "Downward Causation: Polanyi and Prigogine." In *Tradition and Discovery: The Polanyi Society Periodical*, 40:3.

Juarrero, Alicia, 1999. *Dynamics in Action: Intentional Behavior as a Complex System*. MIT Press.

Juarrero, Alicia, 1998. "Causality as Constraint." In van de Vijver, G., Salthe, S.N., Delpos, M. (eds.) *Evolutionary Systems*. Springer. https://doi.org/10.1007/978-94-017-1510-2_17

Juarrero-Roque, Alicia, 1987. "Does Action Theory Rest on a Mistake?" *Philosophy Research Archives* 13: 587–612.

Juarrero, Alicia and C. Rubino, eds. 2010. *Emergence, Complexity and Self-Organization: Precursors and Prototypes*. Emergent Publications.

Kauffman, Stuart, 1993. *Origins of Order: Self-Organization and Selection in Evolution*. Oxford University Press.

Koestler, Arthur, 1968. *The Ghost in the Machine*. Macmillan.

Krishnan, Nikhil, 2023. *A Terribly Serious Adventure: Philosophy and War at Oxford, 1900–1960*. Random House.

Lipscomb, Benjamin J.B., 2021. *The Women are Up to Something: How Elizabeth Anscombe, Philippa Foot, Mary Midgley, and Iris Murdoch Revolutionized Ethics*. Oxford University Press.

Mac Cumhaill, Clare and R. Wiseman, 2022. *Metaphysical Animals: How Four Women Brought Philosophy Back to Life*. Anchor.

MacIntyre, Alasdair, 1981. *After Virtue: A Study in Moral Theory*. University of Notre Dame Press.

Montevil Maël and M. Mossio, 2015. "Biological Organisation as Closure of Constraints." *Journal of Theoretical Biology* 372: 179–191. https://doi.org/10.1016/j.jtbi.2015.02.029

Moore, G.E., 1903. *Principia Ethica*. Cambridge University Press.

Moreno Alvaro and M. Mossio, 2015. *Biological Autonomy: A Philosophical and Theoretical Enquiry*. Springer.

Murdoch, Iris, 1970. "On 'God' and 'Good.'" Chapter in *The Sovereignty of Good*. Routledge.

Murdoch, Iris, 1970. "The Idea of Perfection." Chapter in *The Sovereignty of Good*, 17–28. Routledge.

Murdoch, Iris, 1978. *The Sea, The Sea*. Chatto and Windus.

Nussbaum, Martha, 2011. *Creating Capabilities: The Human Development Approach*. Belknap Press.

Nussbaum, Martha, 2006. *Frontiers of Justice*. Belknap Press.

Nussbaum, Martha 2000. *Women and Human Development: The Capabilities Approach*. Cambridge University Press.

Peirce, Charles Sanders, 1878. "How to Make Our Ideas Clear." *Popular Science Monthly* 12 286: 302.

Prichard, H.A., 1912. Does Moral Philosophy Rest on a Mistake? *Mind* 21, no 81: 21–37.

Rosen, Robert, 1991. *Life Itself*. Columbia University Press.

Ross, W.D., 1930. *The Right and the Good*. Oxford University Press.

Strassler, Matthew. 2024. *Waves in an Impossible Sea: How Everyday Life Emerges from the Cosmic Ocean*. Basic Books.

Varela, Francisco, E. Rosch, and E. Thompson, 1991. *The Embodied Mind: Cognitive Science and Human Experience*. MIT Press.

Whitehead. Alfred North, and B. Russell, 1910–1913. *Principia Mathematica*. Cambridge University Press.

Wittgenstein, Ludwig, 1922. *Tractatus Logico-Philosophicus*. Harcourt, Brace & Co.

Wittgenstein, Ludwig, 1953. *Philosophical Investigations*. Macmillan.

Index

4E Approach, the 17, 59, 134

Abduction 42, 57–58, 92

Adaptation, co-adaptation 22, 68, 133, 150

Absolute Being 24, 29, 35

Action theory 25, 118–119, 123, 134

Agency 17, 24, 27, 52, 111, 117–118, 130–131, 133–134
and human action 17

Analysis, analytic (*see also* reduction and synthesis) 3, 55

Analytic philosophy (*see* ordinary language philosophy)

Anglo-American 5, 8–9, 15, 17, 21, 24, 26, 34, 39, 55–56, 58, 61, 63, 75, 77, 86, 103, 119, 121

Anscombe, Elizabeth 14, 46, 52–53, 79, 85, 96–100, 104–105, 109, 114–126, 130–131, 133–134, 137–138

Anthropology 9, 43, 133

Aristotle
Metaphysics IX 25–27
Nicomachean Ethics 117

Artigiani, Robert 49, 73

Atomism 7, 9, 11, 48–52, 54, 73, 84–85, 91, 101

Attention 98, 102, 114, 128

Attunement (to context) 66–68, 145

Austin, J.L. 75, 79

Autocatalysis, autocatalytic (*see also* catalysis, catalytic) 21, 26, 135, 144

Axiology 11, 16, 67, 68, 107, 109–110, 131

Ayer, Alfred J. 39–40, 48–49, 70–74, 78–79, 81, 96

Barth, John 9

Beauvoir, Simone de 87, 100–101

Bergson, Henri 5, 23

Berlin, Isaiah 6

Big Bang 10, 143–144

Biology 4, 33, 52, 105, 109, 117, 126, 132–134, 136–138

Bohr, Niels 8, 73

Borges, Jorge Luis 9

Born, Max 8, 73
Bottom-up (*see* causation, bottom-up)
Cambridge 36, 63, 77, 79, 88, 89 95, 98–99, 100
Camus, Albert 5–6, 42, 87, 100
Cassirer, Ernst 5, 9, 109
Causation
 Bottom-up 4, 11, 52, 69, 118, 132, 149
 Top-down (versus epiphenomenal) 11, 23, 27, 46–47, 69, 85, 118, 120, 132, 142, 147–150
 Efficient cause (mechanical causes) 7–8, 10, 23, 26, 34, 46, 49, 53, 66, 69–70, 84, 119–121, 138, 140
 Intentional causation 17, 27, 52–53, 85, 116–119, 121–122, 138
 Circular causation (*see also* recursive; *see also* Aristotle) 25–26, 135
 As a category of the understanding (*see* Kant)
 Wayward causal chains 46, 48, 118–119
 Causal singularism 120, 123

Causes versus determinants 54, 118–119, 121
Ceteris paribus laws 109, 124–125
Closure 2, 135, 146, 150–151
Cognitive science 59, 116–117, 122–123
Complexification 10, 143
Complexity, complex systems, complex dynamics 3–4, 10–11, 13, 21–22, 26, 65, 92, 131–132, 134, 136, 139, 142–143, 145, 148–150
Comte, Auguste 6
Conatus 22, 136
Concepts, thick (*see also* Foot) 77, 105–115, 118–120, 123–124, 126, 137–138
Consequentialism 123, 125
Constraints
 Context-dependent 7, 11, 134, 144–145
 Context-independent 143–146, 150
 Enabling 134, 144–145, 149
 Constitutive 147–150
 Governing, second-order 134, 145, 147, 149
 Temporal and spatial 145

Constraint regime (*see also* interdependence) 132, 136, 145, 146–149
Constraint satisfaction 135, 139, 148
Constructivism 5
Context, the lived context 7, 14, 23, 56–57, 92
Context-dependence (*see also* constraints, context-dependent) 5, 7, 9, 59–60, 77, 101, 109–110, 120, 124, 130, 132–133, 139, 146
Continental philosophy 5–8, 26, 42–43, 57, 61, 140
Control, top-down (*see also* mereology) 148, 150
Convection cells 146–148
Coordination 12, 22, 50–51, 92
Cosmos 3, 22, 144, 150
Culture, cultural 1, 4, 11, 24, 31–33, 60–61, 65, 67–69, 76, 85, 113, 126, 130, 132, 134

Deconstruction 5
Deleuze, Gilles 6
Derrida, Jacques 6
Descartes, Rene (Cartesian) 36, 40, 44–45, 51, 53
Dewey, John 42, 59–61

Dissipative structures 142, 145–146, 148
Durkheim, Emile 42

Ecosystems, ecology 1, 4, 12, 21, 67, 130, 132, 134, 136, 138, 142, 147
Einstein, Albert 8, 103, 119
Élan vital (*see* Bergson)
Embeddedness, embedding, embedded 1, 4, 10, 14, 15, 22, 27, 32, 53, 56, 60–61, 65, 67–68, 75, 77, 108–109, 112, 120, 132, 150
Emergent properties, emergent wholes
  Systemic (*see* synchrony, resonance, frequency; *see also* system-wide) 1–3, 10, 15, 21, 67, 130, 135, 138, 140, 143, 150
  As products of constrained relations 11, 145, 147
  As relational properties 23, 49, 90
  As collective properties or dynamics 3, 13, 142
  As interdependent relations 27, 56, 69, 144
Emerson, Ralph Waldo 6, 29–30, 41

Emotivism 70–74, 77–81, 83, 85–86, 96, 99–101, 104–106, 116

Empiricism 34, 44–45, 47–48, 71

Entanglement 8, 47

Environment 1, 3, 12, 14–15, 32, 52, 61, 65, 67, 77, 118–119, 130–133, 139, 148

Environmental ethics 17, 126, 134

Epidemiology 119

Epigenetics 4, 65, 76, 132–133, 145

Epiphenomenal (*see also* causation, top-down) 4, 10, 22, 32, 47, 49, 51–52, 120, 140

Epistemology 5–8, 10, 14, 16, 21, 23–24, 28, 30, 32–33, 38, 48, 50, 52–53, 56, 58, 91, 119, 139, 141, 149

Equilibrium (*see also* metastability) 13, 21–23, 136, 140, 142–143, 146, 148

Essential nature, essentialism 4, 7, 9, 21, 43, 131

Ethology 1, 126, 129, 134

Evolution 22, 67–68, 138, 145, 150

Existentialism 5–6, 38, 42, 83–85, 87, 100–102, 109, 130

Fact–value distinction (*see* Hume; *see* Quine) 15, 53, 63, 71, 73, 77, 79, 100, 105–106, 111, 121, 124, 126, 132, 134, 138–139

Feedback (*see also* recursion) 11, 27, 132, 135, 146, 148

Feyerabend, Paul 6, 115

Fitting together 67–69, 132

Flourishing, human 15, 68, 87, 106, 108–113, 126, 132–133, 138

Foot, Philippa (*nee* Bosanquet) 14, 68, 98–99, 104–115, 119, 121, 123–127, 133–134, 137–138

Forms of life 16, 60, 75–76, 101, 109, 115, 120, 131, 139

Foucault, Michel 6

Fraenkel, Eduard 96

Framing, reframing 32, 35, 58, 61–62, 103

Frege, Gottlob (*see* intuition) 35–39, 44, 66, 74, 86, 89–91

Frequency, as emergent property 1–2

Freud, Sigmund (*see also* superego) 6, 31–34, 41, 61, 101

Geach, Peter 79, 97
Gestalt psychology, gestalts 6, 26, 49, 51–54, 61, 101
Gödel, Kurt 27, 38, 91, 127
Goodness 15, 63–65, 73, 102, 108
Guattari, Félix 6

Habitat 4, 14–15, 61, 67–69, 112, 131–132, 134
Hare, R.M. (*see also* prescriptivism) 79–86, 99–100, 109–110, 123–125, 134, 137
Hartshorne, Charles 43
Hegel, Georg Wilhelm Friedrich 24, 29–30, 35, 38, 41, 86
Heidegger, Martin 5
Heisenberg, Werner 2, 8–9, 73, 91, 145
Heterarchy 139, 143–144, 146–147, 149–150
Hierarchy, as emergent property 2, 139
Holons 2
Homeostasis 2, 4, 51, 147
Hume, David 14, 25, 27, 31, 34, 45, 47–48, 50, 63, 65, 71, 74, 77, 106

Husserl, Edmund (*see also* phenomenology) 5–6, 54–55, 61

Ibsen, Henrik 9, 111
Idealism
  Classical (Plato) 103
  German Absolute Idealism (Hegel) 29–30, 46
  Critical or transcendental idealism (Kant) 24–25, 28, 30–32, 36, 38–40, 69, 82
  British (Bradley, Green) 24, 29, 44–45
  American (Emerson, Thoreau, Royce) 29–30, 44–45
Identity 4, 11–12, 104, 140, 151
Illumination 24, 29–30, 36, 38, 45, 69, 83, 86
Individuation 12, 64
Inference 35, 39, 56–57, 110
Influence
  Contextual 1, 11–12, 25, 32–33, 61, 120, 134, 140, 149
  Structural 1, 16, 69, 85, 113, 151
Information 13, 39, 45–46, 55–56, 64, 109, 136, 142, 145–146

Novelty 1-3, 5, 7, 10, 16, 21-22, 52, 54, 142, 144-145, 147, 149
Nussbaum, Martha 68, 112-114

Observation 10, 38-39, 44-45, 50, 57, 63-64, 71, 81, 83, 136
Ontology 3-4, 8-10, 16, 21, 23, 32-33, 39, 49, 51-54, 56, 65, 84, 91, 103, 119, 120-121, 124, 130, 135-136, 139, 141-142, 145, 149
Ordinary language (analytic) philosophy 9, 39, 59-60, 73, 75-80, 82, 84, 103, 106-110, 114
Organism 4, 15, 21, 51, 107, 131-133, 140, 144, 146-147
Organization (*see also* self-organization) 2, 9-12, 26, 33, 52, 60-61, 65, 68, 85, 111, 113, 131-134, 139, 142-143, 147, 149
Ortega y Gassett, José 6, 43-44
OXFAM 99, 125-126
Oxford 9, 14, 36, 40, 43, 65, 77, 79, 82-84, 88-89, 95-99, 101, 103-105, 109-110, 114, 122, 126, 134, 137

Paradox 8, 38, 71, 90-92, 127
  Cretan liar paradox 90
  Russell's paradox 90
Parameters, order 145-148
Parts-wholes relations (*see* mereology)
Path-dependence 145, 148-149
Patterns 1-2, 13, 22-23, 130, 136, 147
Peirce, Charles Sanders 42, 57-58, 92
Perception, perceptual 25, 29, 30-32, 34, 40-41, 44-46, 48-51, 53-55, 61, 66, 68-71, 74, 101-103, 116-117, 139
  Efficient cause in perception 45-47
Phenomenology 5-6, 30, 54-57, 59-62
Philosophy of science 5, 115
Polanyi, Michael 26
Popper, Karl 6, 91, 115
Positivism 5, 7-8, 10-12, 14-17, 26, 40, 42, 44, 48, 50-51, 55-56, 58, 61-62, 69-70, 72-73, 80, 83, 86, 99-101, 104, 109, 112, 115, 121, 134-135, 137, 143, 150
  Logical positivism 37-39,

41, 45, 47–49, 63, 70, 72, 77, 91, 115
Pragmatism 7, 42, 57–61, 92, 127
Prescriptivism, universal (*see also* R.M. Hare) 66, 70, 79–86, 99–101, 104–106, 108–109
Prichard, H.M. (*see also* intuitionism) 24–25, 44, 65–66, 69, 73, 102
Prigogine, Ilya 142, 146
Principia Mathematica 38, 48, 90–91
Process philosophy 6, 43
Properties, innate (*see* essentialism)

Quantum 8–10, 47
Quine, Willard Van Orman (*see also* fact–value distinction) 39

Realism (*see also* non-naturalism, ethical) 8, 23–24, 28–29, 34, 38–39, 44–47, 49, 53, 56, 63–66, 75
Recursion, recursive 9–10, 25–27, 33, 48, 54, 57, 92, 135, 139, 144
Reduction, reductionism 6–8, 23, 43, 73

Reichenbach, Hans 38
Relations 3, 7, 10–12, 16–17, 21, 25–26, 28, 33, 43, 47, 52–54, 60, 68–69, 77, 85, 111–112, 120–121, 123–126, 132, 134–135, 138–140, 143, 150–151
Resonance, as emergent property 2–3
Rorty, Richard 7, 46
Royce, Josiah 29–30
Russell, Bertrand 36–38, 43, 48, 89–92, 127

Sartre, Jean-Paul 5–6, 9, 42, 87, 101
Self-organization 2, 13, 25–27, 61, 142, 146, 148
  In time (*see also* constraints) 2
  In space (*see also* constraints) 2
Self-reference (*see* paradox)
Semantics 35–36, 39, 75
Sense data, sense datum theory 47–51, 53–54, 57, 59, 66
Sense-making 51, 83, 101, 103–104, 135
Shannon, Claude 39
Smith, Adam 65, 71–72

Sociology 1, 6, 9, 33, 42–43, 60, 108, 115
  Of science 6, 115
Spacetime 9–10, 143–144
Strawson, Peter 79
Structuralism 5, 42
Superego 6, 31–33, 101
  as embedding context, social modulation 32–33
Symbiosis, symbionts 3, 135, 142–143
Synchrony, as emergent property 1–2, 50, 144
Synergies 3, 10, 12–14, 51, 131, 142, 144–146
System-wide (*see also* emergent systemic) 3, 21, 67–69, 135, 143

Teleology, as self-organization (*see also* Kant) 25–26
Theory of mind 68
Thermodynamics 10, 13, 136, 140, 142, 146, 149
Thoreau, Henry David 6, 29–30, 41, 128
Tillich, Paul 87
Timing (*see also* constraints, temporal, context-dependent) 4, 9, 50–51, 144–145

Tolstoy, Leo 9
Top-down (*see* causation, top-down)
Transcendental Categories of the Understanding 30, 32–33, 35, 40, 46, 86
Transcendentalism 30, 41
Turing, Alan 27, 91–92

Umwelt 14, 69, 109, 132
Unamuno, Miguel de 6, 43
Utilitarianism 64

Validity versus soundness (sound, unsound) 37, 40
Values 11–12, 16, 22, 24–25, 65, 74, 77, 85, 132, 134, 138, 147
Verification, principle of (*see also* positivism) 39, 46–48, 50–52, 72–73, 83, 91
Vienna Circle (*see also* positivism) 34–40, 48, 50
Virtue ethics 17, 112, 114, 134
Virtues
  Classical 106, 112, 114, 132
  Prudence 106
  Courage 105–107
  Temperance 106

Weber, Max 12
Whitehead, Alfred North 6, 26, 38, 43, 48, 90

Wholes–parts relations (*see* mereology)
World War I 36, 64, 70, 77, 88, 96
World War II 14, 40, 73–75, 77–79, 86–89, 95, 101, 137
Wittgenstein, Ludwig 16, 36, 40, 60, 75, 79, 99, 101, 105, 109, 115, 118, 124, 131

www.ingramcontent.com/pod-product-compliance
Lightning Source LLC
Chambersburg PA
CBHW070944230426
43666CB00011B/2554